Linda Anderson

W9-ATK-801

LEADERSHIP SKILLS

Developing Volunteers for Organizational Success

by Emily Kittle Morrison

FISHER BOOKS

Publishers: Helen V. Fisher
                 Howard W. Fisher
                 Fred W. Fisher
                 J. McCrary

Editor: Fred W. Fisher

Book Designer: Edgar H. Allard
Cover Designer: Paula K. Peterson

Published by Fisher Books
4239 W. Ina Road, Suite 101
Tucson, AZ 85741
(602) 744-6110

All rights reserved. With the exception of forms designed to be copied by the user, no other part of this book may be reproduced or transmitted in any form or by any means, electronic or mechanical, including photocopy, recording or any information storage or retrieval system, without written permission from the publisher, except by a reviewer who may quote brief passages.

**Library of Congress
Cataloging-in-Publication Data**
Morrison, Emily K. (Emily Kittle)
    Leadership Skills: Developing
    Volunteers for Organizational Success
    by Emily Kittle Morrison.
    p. cm.
    Rev. ed. of: Working with Volunteers.
    Includes bibliographical references
    (p. 240) and index.

ISBN 1-55561-066-8 $16.95

    Voluntarism - - United States - - Management. 2. Leadership. 3. Associations, institutions, etc. - - United States - - Personnel management. 4. Volunteers - - United States. I. Morrison, Emily K. (Emily Kittle). Working with Volunteers. II. Title.

HN90.V64M67 1994
361.3'7 - - dc20   94-9333
                                        CIP

© 1983, 1988, 1994, Emily K. Morrison

Printed in United States of America
Printing 10 9 8 7 6 5 4 3 2

Notice: The information in this book is true and complete to the best of our knowledge. It is offered with no guarantees on the part of the author or Fisher Books. The author and publisher disclaim all liability in connection with the use of this book.

Fisher Books are available at special quantity discounts for educational use. Special books, or book excerpts, can also be created to fit specific needs. For details please write or telephone.

Acknowledgments

Over the duration of four printings of this book many people have offered their help. My first words of thanks are to my family for the patience and encouragement.

Additionally, Libby Kittle, Amanda Place, Linda Waldrop, Ann Bannard and Edgar Allard all offered insight and assistance.

Besides these, I am indebted to the many bright and creative trainers from whom I have learned and with whom I have worked.

Contents

Introduction

"A Leader is best when people barely know he exists."
—Lao Tse

Leadership Skills is a handbook for volunteers and their leaders. This new format and revision of my earlier *Working with Volunteers: Skills for Leadership* has been developed to facilitate your learning as a reader.

The information is presented so you can consult a pertinent chapter as the material is needed. You will not find *all* the answers; nor are these the *only* answers. These are concepts I believe to be useful, workable and wise.

The book is not meant to be all-inclusive, nor original. Contained within these pages are tools for success. To what extent you find these concepts useful, or even agree with them, will depend on your background and perspective.

Twenty-five years as a national leadership development trainer have given me considerable insight into not only the concerns of volunteer leaders but what works. I have spent the last decade researching such things as factors affecting loyalty in non-profit agencies and human-resource management.

Leaders in the not-for-profit arena, as in the corporate world, need to view each challenge with a view of *possibility*. The very nature of the resource—the volunteer—demands that a leader be a *nurturer*. A leader's main function is to show appreciation. Volunteers work for 'good feelings', not paychecks, perks and parking spaces.

Clear vision is important. A demonstrated commitment is essential. A sense of team is basic. But unless a volunteer leader continually recognizes and acknowledges the contributions of their volunteers, the success of their projects is likely to be limited. No task is more important than the people involved.

Positions of leadership bring a certain potential for power and control. The challenge is to remember that the misuse of these will drive people away. People want to be 'asked', not 'told'. People expect to be asked to think, not just listen and obey.

The misuse of leadership and its implicit power will lead to three predictable responses. Followers will *fight*. When pushed they will push back. Those who do not like fighting will take *flight*. They will simply leave. And, finally, the meek will *submit*. Chances are they will not contribute enthusiastically, they will simply follow orders and wait for the task to be completed. They may leave at the first opportunity.

Effective leaders *listen*. Effective leaders tune into and care about the views, biases, values and perspectives of those they work with. Effective leaders recognize that these are *their* realities. The views of some may not be based on facts, but they affect people's responses. An effective leader will confront differences in a non-accusatory fashion. His or her aim is to clarify misconceptions.

The material in this book provides you, the volunteer leader, access to important key concepts. It can serve as a guide book for officers, a handbook for committee chairmen and a training manual for potential leaders and provisionals in community groups.

Community board members can use it as a reference for challenges in group planning. Business leaders will find suggestions for dealing with motivation and communication. Effective leadership skills are quite similar at work or in the community. Not-for-profit agencies and organizations are charged with staying in the black, that is to say they must spend funds wisely. To do this they need effective, skilled leaders.

The ultimate success of any organization, community or corporation, will hinge on the skills of those in positions of leadership, how they execute their power, how loose their rein, how empowering their control. Customer satisfaction and customer service mean concerns for the constituent as well as the client. This concern provided the focus for this book.

How to Use This Book

All the information, checklists and guidelines included in this book are for your use. I hope you will adapt, edit, reproduce and recreate those materials that look like they might help your organization. These forms and key concepts can be included in a Board Orientation packet, used as handouts in skill workshops or adapted as worksheets for sessions designed to facilitate discussion, to problem-solve, or to establish new direction.

Highlights and specific points can be used graphically on flip charts or transparencies as visual aids in training sessions with staff, Boards, and volunteers.

It is not necessary to request specific permission to use these materials for any non-profit endeavor. However, a note of credit to the source may prove useful later on, and would be considerate to my contributors.

Volunteers

"Get Your Good Feelings"

*"What I spent, is gone
what I kept, is lost
but what I gave to charity
will be mine forever"*
—Epitaph

Some things that belong to us that are so precious we can't sell them; we must share them with others. So it is with your volunteer efforts.

There is a certain reward in being a part of an effort that makes a difference. In contemporary society the problems are complex, the solutions more involved and the satisfactions more obscure. These challenges spark the interest and involvement of 20th-century volunteers. This involvement meets inner needs and brings happiness.

"Happiness is the utilization of one's talents along lines of excellence"
—Aristotle

TRENDS IN VOLUNTARISM

Today a far greater percentage of the population is involved in volunteer efforts than at any time in history. A new consciousness of domestic deprivation, the beginning of racial militancy and rising affluence (permitting increased leisure), have all affected voluntarism.

Many customary recipients of volunteer services are now serving their own community—the young, the old, the handicapped and the poor. Voluntarism now includes every economic group.

PERIODS OF TRANSITION
Colonization and Survival

Four transition periods brought us where we are today in American voluntarism. The first was Colonization. Voluntarism was necessary for survival. Church work, town councils and barn raisings are examples.

Organized Progress

The second period was the Civil War through the 1930s. Voluntarism changed from individual charity to organized programs (Red Cross, YWCA, Hull House, Salvation Army, Boy Scouts, Goodwill, etc.). World War I saw the beginning of domestic issues and the establishment of the American Hearing Society, Crippled Children Society, Foundation for the Blind. And the Depression brought local relief activities. Community Chest, charities and service became Big Business.

Middle Class

The third was a change from an upper-class activity to that of the middle class: the establishment of March of Dimes and other nickel-and-dime collections, and such things as payroll deductions. World War II brought staggering growth: health and welfare organizations and door-to-door fund raising began in earnest.

Finally the fourth: Participatory Democracy. Voluntarism began to represent all segments of society and with it came the birth of self-help groups.

OVERVIEW

The tradition of volunteering evolved not just from altruism but a combination of religious spirit (of man's humanity to man) and a dose of mutual dependence and assistance.

"To portray your history as though it were related solely to goodness of heart may describe the best in your forefathers, but would not identify the widespread tradition of organized neighborliness which hardship dictated and goodness tempered."*

Our country has survived and flourished in great part because of the concern and caring of people in every community. The culture, life style and freedom Americans enjoy have allowed individuals the opportunity to invest their time and energy on causes of their choosing. The efforts of caring people have made substantial differences in the quality of life in our towns and cities. Individuals can, and do, make a difference.

An 'Action Orientation' was the focus of the '50s. The current thrust is toward 'Advocacy': speaking up and lobbying for causes and concerns. However, most voluntary organizations still spend considerable time and effort 'doing'.

*Brian O'Connell *Effective Leadership in Voluntary Organizations*, Follett Publications, Chicago, © 1981.

More and more efforts are being exercised to form coalitions, to collaborate, and to "network" with other organizations and agencies. The attempt is to avoid the duplication of time, money and manpower. The National Center for Citizen Involvement is a fine example (on a national scale) of sharing ideas and resources. In communities all across the country, groups are beginning to work together to bring about change. They are sharing office space, phone lines, address lists, manpower and expertise.

For effectiveness and efficiency, groups would be wise to recognize the importance of needs assessment, training and evaluation. I have a strong bias for the investment in ongoing skill development and assessment of current effectiveness in meeting needs and objectives.

Nothing is constant but change itself. Because of this a consciousness must be raised in volunteer leaders for the ever-changing needs of constituents, clients and volunteers.

Beyond these more immediate concerns, there are broad-based concerns for the future. These include:

+ State and local ordinances that limit an organization's ability to function

+ Tax-exemption restrictions

+ IRS accounting that can be confusing

+ Conservatism

+ Congressional proposals which could limit activities (such as student activism)

+ Tax laws that discourage charitable giving

+ Federal restrictions on public-interest law firms

+ The need to be adequately insured

+ The trend toward mandated voluntary service

In a country based on the belief in freedom, government should be involved (in voluntarism) only to the extent that it preserves the rights and freedoms which allow volunteer activities to flourish.

FOCUS ON VOLUNTARISM

Who Volunteers and Why?

A wider variety of people than ever before can be found to be actively involved in voluntary pursuits.

✤ **Unemployed Middle-Class Women**—probably always will volunteer to demonstrate a commitment to their community, to advance causes they care about, as well as for for purely social reasons.

✤ **Employed and Professional People**—always have volunteered to challenge talents and skills untapped on the job—because it is "good business."

✤ **Retired People**—volunteer more than ever. We are a healthier nation and our senior citizens are filled with ability, interest and life. Volunteering allows them to continue to feel needed (which they are!)

✤ **Teenagers**—volunteer to gain a sense of self-worth, to develop skills, and to demonstrate their dependability and initiative (supervisors are great references for real jobs). And many volunteer jobs lead to paid jobs, if just through "contacts."

✤ **The Unemployed**—volunteer to make these same kinds of contacts, as a form of career development, and to diminish the negative feelings which accompany the state of unemployment.

✤ **The Needy**—volunteer more and more self-help groups are springing up within communities and sub-groups. Many organizations ask that clients invest time in exchange for services.

✤ **Preschoolers**—Some Veterans' Hospitals have Moppet Programs that train and involve little people in activities in the Geriatric Ward. It is good for everyone.

✤ **Newcomers**—to make friends and to become involved in the new communities—usually associating with an organization that interested them back home, but just as often with the one that reaches out and makes them feel welcomed.

EFFECTS OF ECONOMIC POLICIES ON VOLUNTARISM

✤ **Presidential belief** in the potential of volunteers has been significant in raising the consciousness of the country to the possibility of making a difference through voluntary action. This has given the volunteer some prestige. It's hard to look down on a whole segment of the population that a President has praised.

✤ **Federal cutbacks** create a great need to provide services that have come to be expected (that were formerly provided by the government). Economic conditions and policies always create the framework in which voluntarism takes place.

✤ **Budget cuts** cause agencies and organizations to fill in for dollars that government previously provided to assist in their program delivery.

❖ **Service reduction,** as well as support money, affect the volunteer commitment needed to continue activities from research to hot meals.

❖ **The "Philosophy of Entitlement"** has raised a generation to "expect" that someone (else) will provide them with many things in their lives.

❖ **Advocacy efforts**—individuals and groups are speaking out for causes and changes they believe in.

❖ **The dollar value of volunteer time** in 1990 was over $64 billion. The combined money contribution of individuals, corporations and foundations—(nearly $4 billion according to a study by The Independent Sector) is likely to go down as inflation cuts into discretionary income and tax laws discourage contributions.

FUTURE LEADERSHIP
What Organizations can do to Assure Future Leadership

❖ Percentages—52% of all U. S. citizens over 13 (according to The Gallup Poll) volunteer in some manner. 84 million are associated with structured programs such as Scouting and Red Cross. The higher the education level the higher the number of hours (as well as dollars) donated. Time donated will continue at about the same level, though the mix of *who* is volunteering is changing.

❖ First and primarily, organizations must recognize the need for continuing education. This is in part because of perpetual changes (particularly in personnel, which we must expect in any nonprofit organization). It is also because each new experience we have in life prepares people for different things.

❖ Assure effectiveness, and leadership. Recognize that an orientation should be presented annually. Even if the manpower or Board happens to remain basically the same (very unlikely)—the situation and direction change. Those responsible for these changes should have a chance to clarify their expectations and to understand the expectations of co-workers.

❖ Focus as much attention on the *process* and the people as typically given to the *task*. Recognize the potential of new volunteers and provide avenues for development. Allow for committee assignments, then co-chairmanships, then chairmanships and Board positions. This experience helps build Leadership.

❖ Part of Leadership comes from a confidence level felt within (because of feeling a part of a group, and being capable of handling the situations and the people). A conscious effort should be made to develop a sense of team within the group. Learn about people as talented individuals beyond their role in the group.

✤ Interactive meetings allow members of the group to feel they are truly a part of things and that their feelings are heard. In terms of Leadership development, the task of "facilitator" can be rotated so each member has a chance to lead. (see Chapter 2, *Meetings*.)

✤ A good entrance interview and wise placement can put you in touch with the abilities of the volunteers. A periodic "needs assessment" will keep you current as to the motivation and areas of interest of each member so he or she can be challenged and his or her retention better assured. Skill banks are wonderful tools for staying on top of where the talent is. They help you know where to go when your organization has specific needs.

✤ Expecting that those around you "bring solutions not problems" to your attention allows members to develop skills within themselves rather than looking to others for answers.

✤ A policy that discourages members from serving more than two consecutive terms on a Board will challenge you to look for new people. Typically Board members are the group's happiest. Increase the percentage of your members who get Board experience.

RESOURCES

There are resources in the community to help agencies and organizations in training their volunteers.

Trainers

Local and National leadership development trainers periodically offer training sessions to the public. There are also workshops designed for specific groups to deal with their personnel and specific interests. The American Society for Training and Development is composed of individuals working in the Human Resource Development field. Though primarily professionals with major corporations, it is possible to get assistance through this organization.

National Speakers Association

The National Speakers Association is made up of many talented individuals prepared to address organizations on a wide range of topics, beginning with Motivation.

Junior Leagues

The Association of Junior Leagues has as its purpose: To demonstrate the effectiveness of trained volunteers. To this end they often have among their services to the community a program which provides trainers willing to offer various workshops on Management and Leadership.

Collaborations

Organizations such as United Way, Girl Scouts, the Y, Red Cross and others have long realized the need for training. I would like to see more cooperation among agencies to share experts and to offer training sessions to others.

Pfeiffer & Company   Pfeiffer & Company of San Diego, California, produces wonderful manuals for training that can serve as guides to organizations interested in developing their own training resources.

Associations   Associations such as Volunteer, DOVIA (Directors of Volunteers in Agencies) and the AVA (Association of Volunteer Administrators) are all helpful resources devoted to voluntarism.

Libraries   Libraries are filled with material from management to motivation. Though much is designed for business, the concepts are transferable to the volunteer setting.

Books   This book is a handbook of checklists and guidelines, filled with key concepts for consideration. Other such books are available through the National Center for Citizen Involvement in Arlington, Virginia.

Audio and Video Tapes   More and more audio and video tapes are being produced that profile concrete suggestions for use in training sessions. Some are recorded during national conference presentations. Others are produced strictly as training tools.

Magazines   *Training Magazine*, the *Training and Development Journal* (of the American Society for Training and Development), *Leadership, Voluntary Action Leadership, The Journal of Volunteer Administration* (published by the Association of Volunteer Administrators) all provide up-to-the minute concepts, suggestions and statistics.

STAFF TRAINING   What about staff? Remember that they too need training in how to deal effectively with volunteers.

+ All of your efforts in recruiting and training can be for naught if the volunteer must work with a staff person who views him as an aggravation.

+ The staff should be shown just how volunteers can augment the work. There should also be an awareness of the fact that what they do and how they do it affects the volunteer.

+ Staff is generally responsible for the atmosphere of any agency. Is it one in which an individual whose primary motivation is "psychic income" (good feelings) could thrive?

+ Staff should be involved in the team-building efforts, and helped to realize that **volunteers do not threaten their jobs.** If a staff job is eliminated it says more about the economy than anything else. If they are eased out it is probably because of their inability to handle the job or get along with the co-workers; not because a volunteer is in the wings.

✦ Volunteers do not take jobs away from a community. They are doing tasks that either would not get done (Little League, Girl Scouts, 4-H, Junior Achievement, Meals on Wheels, etc.) or would have to be handled by an individual already overburdened. They often create jobs through innovative projects.

✦ The fact that volunteers are putting in hours in no way affects the rate of unemployment. As a matter of fact, a great percentage of volunteers (particularly Board members) are people who work full time and give volunteer time in addition.

✦ Staff needs to be included in planning sessions. They need to be a part of decisions that affect them. They need to feel they are a part of things, that they are needed and appreciated. They must realize they serve as the "constant" in an otherwise changing situation. Day after day volunteers come and go, do what they can and leave. Staff remains, providing invaluable continuity.

✦ Everyone involved should have an annual review of the goals and objectives of the organization and how they affect the staff and volunteers. What is expected of each should be clarified with all concerned.

✦ Staff should be actively involved in developing the job descriptions for volunteers who will work under their supervision.

✦ Many a dedicated, dependable volunteer has moved on to another agency for lack of understanding, sympathy, or appreciation by staff. You can't share from an empty cup—these staff people must first feel good about themselves and what they are doing.

✦ Training is needed on all levels. Even those of us who train, if we're good and care, continue to participate in training sessions developed by others and to increase our knowledge and expertise.

JOB DESCRIPTIONS AND CONTRACTS

Job descriptions for volunteers and an agreed-upon contract can help facilitate the activities of an organization. They help to assure satisfaction for the volunteer and to clarify the expectations held by all.

GUIDELINES FOR VOLUNTEERS

Volunteers are people who give of their time in service to their community. In addition, they have a unique opportunity to serve as interpreters between the community and its agencies.

✓ Carefully choose the area in which you wish to work. Jobs suited to your interest and abilities are likely to be the most rewarding.

✓ Realistically estimate the amount of time you have to give. Time commitments should be honored.

✓ Always arrive at assignments at the agreed time. If you must be absent, call as early as possible to be excused. If feasible, you should provide substitutes.

✓ Have a clear understanding of what your roles and duties are. Request a written job description. Volunteers should expect continued guidance and direction.

✓ Expect to participate in an orientation session and any offered training programs. If you find your time is not well spent, discuss the situation with the person in charge.

✓ Respect the principle of confidentiality and follow the same ethical standards expected of all staff members.

✓ Approach the working situation with an open mind. If you do not understand or agree with any procedure, ask questions.

DEDUCTIONS

The cost of transportation from a volunteer's home to where he serves is deductible. Keep track of your mileage and figure credit according to current IRS guidelines (available from the IRS). Other items usually covered include:

✦ Reasonable cost for meals and lodging

✦ The cost of attending a religious conference as a delegate

✦ Cost of upkeep of uniforms

✦ Unreimbursed expenses directly connected with and solely attributable to voluntary service performed for one's church or synagogue

✦ Use of personal auto, gas and oil or standard mileage for parking and toll fees

✦ Travel expenses in excess of allowance provided

Actual deductions will differ with each agency due to policies and budgets. Considerable lobbying is being done nationally to try to affect overall rules and regulations in this area. Contact your nearest IRS office for current rulings.

CONSIDERATIONS FOR A VOLUNTEER CONTRACT

❖ Spell out the agency's expectations for the volunteer's participation (including such things as uniforms and number of hours).

❖ Delineate the responsibilities of the volunteer for specific assignments (as seen by the agency).

❖ Establish limits of authority, as well as the lines of authority for the volunteer. Describe any liability he or she could face.

❖ Indicate the area of support that will be provided by the agency to the volunteer, such as orientation and training.

❖ Clarify the extent to which volunteer expenses are covered by the agency, well as how to record expenses for personal tax credit.

Additional Objectives

❖ The contract should be designed to meet the specific needs of the agency. It may vary for different types of volunteers within the organization.

❖ This tool should be filled out *together,* so that any area of confusion can be clarified immediately.

❖ It should be a tool of assistance and assurance that the needs of both the volunteer and the agency will be met. It should not been seen as something which will be "held over" a willing volunteer.

❖ It can be an effective device for both Leadership and Career Development.

❖ A "gratuitous employee" is one working under direction and with supervision of action controlled by an agency or organization—without remuneration. Defined working limits are encouraged to establish responsibility in case of an accident or law suit.

GUIDELINES FOR VOLUNTEER CONTRACT

Agency Name_____ **Form #**_____

Date_____

Agency Volunteer

Name: _____ Social Security # _____
       LAST   FIRST   MIDDLE

Address: _____ Date of Birth: _____ Sex: ____
                                          MONTH/DAY/YEAR

Phone: _____ Home Work _____

Organization represented (if applicable):_____

Current occupation: _____

Previous volunteer experience: _____

Applicable professional experience: _____

Applicable educational background: _____

Particular interests or hobbies:_____

Why would you like to volunteer here?_____

What type of service would you prefer? _____

Please indicate the days of the week and hours you could serve: _____

Day: _____ From: _____ To: _____ | Time Limit of Commitment _____

Day: _____ From: _____ To: _____ | _____

Do you have a current driver's license? #_____ Chauffeur's? # _____

Do you have transportation? _____ Could you furnish it for others? _____

Do you have minimum automobile insurance required by law? _____

In case of emergency, please notify: _____

   Address _____ Phone: _____

Job description:_____

Supervisor: _____ Phone: _____

Areas of responsibility: _____

Limit of authority: _____

Specific expectations:_____

Assigned schedule: Day:_____ From: _____ To:_____

                      Day: _____ From: _____ To: _____

Where you can go for help: _____

Orientation program: Date: _____ Time: _____Place: _____

Training available: _____

(If confidentiality is involved, a paragraph of policy would be
appropriate, as would guidelines about dealing with the press).

_____

_____

_____

Signed: _____   _____
               VOLUNTEER   SUPERVISOR

Date: _____   Date: _____

2

Meetings

"Haven't we met before?"

Meetings are often held by committees and this is where the real business takes place. Board and organizational decisions are based on the transactions in committee meetings. F. Allen has been quoted to say a committee is "A group of the unprepared, appointed by the unwilling, to do the unnecessary." If this is true, no wonder people complain about meetings!

GUIDELINES FOR CALLING A MEETING
Before having a committee meeting be sure that it is a committee that is truly needed. If it is, realistic objectives can be set. The chairman should have a job description that makes sense. He or she should follow some basic guidelines when calling any meeting. These include to:

✤ State the reason for the meeting (on an agenda form, postcard, or at least in a call to the participants).

✤ Set the standard (by arriving on time and coming prepared).

✤ Develop an awareness of group dynamics (seek to make everyone comfortable and feel a part).

✤ Arrange for a written report of the transactions for the record (whether formal minutes, an interaction memo or simply a set of notes in a notebook).

Communicate! Far too often meetings and subcommittee meetings are held, grand and wonderful plans made, and actions taken. But there is little or no communication with others in the organization who may be affected by the decisions. Always keep the executive body apprised of your activities to coordinate efforts among committees. Notify the membership at large, preferably through a newsletter, but at least at the general membership meeting.

MEETING CONSIDERATIONS Before ever calling a meeting, the committee or Board Chairman should give serious thought to why it is needed and what needs to be accomplished. Time invested in advance of the meeting will save time during the meeting. It will help assure that the time invested is productive.

✤ What are the needs, interests and expectations of the participants?

✤ What is the agreed-upon purpose of the meeting? (to train, inform, plan, decide, etc.)

✤ What materials are needed to facilitate the meeting? (who will handle them? agenda, handouts, visual aids, etc.)

✤ Are additional resource people needed? (who? who will contact them?)

✤ What activities can best be used to achieve the stated goal? (brainstorming, survey, discussion, buzz sessions, etc.)

✤ Is there enough time beforehand for everyone to prepare adequately?

✤ How much time will be needed to deal with the issues? (Plan the agenda with consideration for this).

✤ What commitments do you seek and from whom?

✤ Where could the meeting most effectively take place? (home, office, conference room, on site)

✤ Who will be responsible for room arrangements, refreshments, clean up? (secure commitment)

RESPONSIBILITIES OF THE CHAIRMAN

Objectives Plan meetings in relation to objectives. Good leadership begins before the meeting with plans for time, method and resources for accomplishing the stated goals.

Expectations Plan meetings in relation to what members expect. A well-planned agenda is essential, but success depends on the participants having the information in advance, with time to prepare.

Goals   Open with a review of the meeting's purpose. Define and clarify goals during the meeting. Without a clear understanding of the direction the meeting is to take, problems are likely to develop. Members may become bogged down in unrelated discussion.

Appraise   Appraise progress mid-stream. It is never too late to choose a new direction. It is important that everyone understand what has been done and what remains ahead, who is responsible and what the deadlines are (see Objective Setting, page 139). Periodic progress reports are useful.

Procedures Use suitable methods of procedure (see Chapter 9, *Problem-Solving*). It is important to address problems from the most realistic approach. Different circumstances lend themselves to different approaches.

Evaluate   Evaluation doesn't mean to be critical of the people or of yourself. It means to consider the *process* critically to determine its effectiveness or lack of it.

Communicate Make it a habit to use active listening techniques (see Chapter 8, *Listening*) to assure that what you are saying is what you mean, and what is being heard is what you intended.

Decisions Determine "decision-readiness." Use caution before calling for a vote. The group may have too little information or feel unsure of its implication. Premature action may also come about if the leader fails to bring out the unexpressed inner concerns of reticent members. Dissatisfaction may follow.

Delegate   Create new jobs as needs arise. An effective leader realizes when it is time to create a new job, (with appropriate recognition). Many responsibilities are best delegated. A reasonable division of labor will ease the pressure on currently involved members. It will offer opportunities to others for involvement and growth.

Conflicts Discuss problems openly. Conflicts or anxieties should be acknowledged openly and discussed frankly. To accomplish tasks efficiently the *process* must be effective. Face tension squarely (see Chapter 12, *Conflict Management*). The surface reason for tension may actually camouflage the real reasons. Every attempt should be made to air these concerns.

Climate   Set a climate of free expression. People are more apt to express themselves honestly in an atmosphere of informality, friendliness and mutual respect (see Chapter 5, *Leadership*). When members feel inhibited, or lack confidence or trust in the group or the leader, the session has less chance of being successful.

GUIDELINES FOR COMMITTEE CHAIRMEN

An effective leader will help empower those willing to take on some of the responsibility for the success of programs and projects. A committee chairman needs to give serious consideration to activities that will help facilitate the effectiveness of the group. The following points are offered as a guideline.

1. **Provide an orientation session for your members**
   - ✓ Allow time to get to know one another
     (see Team Building Exercises and Icebreakers in Chapter 3, *Board Skills*)
   - ✓ Discuss your purpose and policies
   - ✓ Explain committee structure and responsibilities
   - ✓ Clarify goals and agree upon objectives
     (see Chapter 11, *Quality Management*)

2. **Mail a prepared agenda in advance of your meeting**
   - ✓ Allow time for unfinished business
   - ✓ List reports and who is responsible
   - ✓ Schedule time with flexibility
   - ✓ Carefully consider the order in which you place business on the agenda

3. **During Meeting**
   - ✓ Arrive early
   - ✓ Begin on time (be sure a quorum is present)
   - ✓ Keep the meeting moving and be sensitive to the needs of the group to be heard
   - ✓ Keep the discussion on track and clarify frequently (or help the facilitator to do this)

   Motions should state:
   - ✓ what is to be done
   - ✓ at what cost
   - ✓ by whom
   - ✓ a prescribed time limit

   Be cautious not to tie yourself down with unneeded specifics.

4. **When possible, set meeting dates well in advance** (so your project has priority on each member's calendar). An annual calendar developed with all involved can assure better attendance.

5. **Do not call unneeded meetings**

HOW TO ARRANGE AN AGENDA

The preparation of an agenda must be specific enough to make it truly useful to the participants. To simply list such things as New Business and Old Business really tells nothing. A well-conceived agenda fully prepares the group for the business at hand and assures an expedient and productive meeting.

Sending out the agenda in advance allows participants to come prepared in spirit and with needed materials. The members are then mentally ready for the discussions and prepared with information or supplies appropriate to the issues. A chairman has a better chance of conducting a successful meeting if she sets the stage and reminds her Board or committee that she expects them to take time to review the agenda.

An itemized agenda helps the chairman or facilitator to stay on track and on time. The members should understand that you intend to stick by the time frames (unless the group as a whole chooses to alter the framework). Anticipating the possible reaction to each item by the group gives the chairman a chance to balance the issues on the agenda.

Matters of extreme importance or emotion generate the greatest reactions and are often most time-consuming. Each of these concerns should be considered when establishing an agenda so one heated item does not run right after another.

If the issues to be covered require a degree of knowledge this information should be provided in advance. An example of this could be an attached sheet listing Pros and Cons to a proposal. Additionally, if a committee has fully researched a question and is ready to bring a proposal for action to the Board for a vote, a brief background sheet should be included. This highlights the points of significance in the proposal.

CONSIDERATIONS FOR AN ACTION AGENDA

✤ State clearly what you expect to accomplish (the purpose of the meeting)

✤ Specify a definitive amount of time for each item

✤ Indicate *who* will be responsible as a resource for each item

✤ Open with items of special interest and end with items worth staying to hear

✤ Avoid
  ✓ Two time-consuming items in a row
  ✓ Two items of high emotion back-to-back
  ✓ Two similar subjects, one after the other
  ✓ Two routine items in a row
  ✓ Non-action items which can be covered in writing (attached to the Consent Agenda)

The idea is to balance the agenda, to maintain interest and to encourage promptness and serious consideration of *all* significant items. Careful attention should be given to each item to determine whether it is appropriate to the meeting. Some concerns are better dealt with on a lower level.

A well-designed agenda allows for *anyone* to facilitate the meeting. The responsibility lies with the Chairman to specify clearly what she hopes to cover, in what time frame. She should also encourage the commitment of each member to commit each member to active participation.

She can provide needed background material and serve as a resource for the discussion.

An Action Agenda is appropriately the second portion of any Consent Agenda. The Consent Agenda facilitates the decision-making of routine or clear-cut issues. Treasurers' reports and minutes need not take up meeting time being read aloud. These things can be attached to the agenda or mailed with the Consent Agenda. They should be considered in advance of the meeting. Any corrections or additions can quickly be made prior to approval.

THE CONSENT AGENDA

Items that require full involvement and final action should appear with specific time frames suggested. The **action** part of any meeting is the real reason for convening the session—not to simply *report* what could be read at leisure and filed for future reference. The background, reference and quick attention items become part of the Consent Agenda.

The Consent Agenda is a time-saving tool that assures accuracy and opens up participation and communication. It is sent in advance of the meeting. It is *consent* because the participants of the meeting *consent* to accept:

✓ The minutes (Group Memo, page 22), that are *attached* can be dealt with by correction or addition and a quick vote, but need *not* be read.

✓ The Treasurer's report, that can be attached and dealt with similarly.

✓ Proposals that require a quick vote. The item is presented in exact wording and background information is included.

✓ The responsibility for coming prepared to deal with issues listed and having given advance thought to each item. Participants are obliged to come prepared with items requested (i.e., "please bring") and are the responsible for coming fully prepared to discuss issues they have said they would present at the meeting. With the Consent Agenda participants agree to the time frame presented, or to mutually agree to alter it.

This approach is most useful when used with an Interaction Meeting which involves a Facilitator and Recorder. It has a common focus by using a flip chart on which information is recorded with markers.

Ripple Effect

A meeting can have a ripple effect in that each person attending takes positive or negative reactions from that meeting. If the response is anger or frustration these feelings can then be taken out on family or co-workers. Their anger and frustration is one of the costs of an unsuccessful meeting!

By the same token, an effective meeting can have great benefits. Participants can return home or to their job rejuvenated and happily motivated. Their good feelings can be shared much in the same way that "courtesy is contagious." With improved meeting skills come improved team work, communication, morale and productivity.

CONSENT AGENDA FORM

Committee Name: _____

Date: _____

Place: _____   *(directions if necessary)*

Time: _____   *(beginning and ending)*

Facilitator: _____

Recorder: _____

Refreshments:_____

What to Bring: _____

_____

_____

What We Need to Accomplish: _____

_____

_____

Time should be assigned to each issue and the person's name listed for those responsible for background material. Yellow line the name when sending to the individual committed.

Action Items (Action Agenda)

Such as:	9:00	Coffee and informal time
	9:15	Team-building exercise—name
	9:30	First item—name
	10:00	Second item—name
	10:45	Third item—name
	11:15	Fourth item—name
	11:45	Establish next step (future plans)
		Assign individuals responsible
	12:00	Adjourn

Special Notes:_____

_____

Resource Persons: _____

_____

© 1994 Emily Kittle Morrison, *Leadership Skills*, Fisher Books, Tucson, Arizona

Effective Facilitator   The ripple effect takes place simply because any process affects all who become involved, directly or indirectly. The aim of a good facilitator is to 'ease' the situation, to 'facilitate', to help good things happen. An effective facilitator works at all times to remain neutral. He protects all participants, helps everyone to be heard accurately, clarifies and seeks consensus. The Ripple Effect will register positively on the organization's effectiveness long after the close of a meeting.

GROUP INTERACTION   If it distresses you that meetings never start on time, get sidetracked, and are inaccurately recorded, here are a few tricks of the trade.

The only way to start a meeting on time is to *start it when you said you would*. Gain a reputation for standing by the hour stated even if you must build in some social time: 9:15 coffee, 9:30 introductions. State it in your agenda and **Stick To It!**

This section is really about how to conduct a meeting so that the group is with you. It is a technique called *Interaction*.

INTERACTION MEETINGS*   Interactive meetings differ from regular meetings in a number of ways. I think you will find the approach more user-friendly and more attuned to the needs and wishes of the participants. If Board and Committee Chairmen truly seek a "buy-in" of the membership, this technique is more apt to produce it than a formal, Parliamentary meeting.

Interaction	**Parliamentary Procedure**
more informal, effective in smaller groups	formal, designed for large groups
leadership functions divided between chairman and facilitator	chairman is responsible for both content and process of meeting
stresses consensus and win/win decision making	uses majority vote, leading to win/lose decisions
recorder and group memory makes progress of the meeting visible and self-correcting	secretary takes notes privately for later use
group memo summarizes notes made and corrected at meeting	minutes written by a single member of the group, corrected at next meeting

*Based on material by Doyle, Michael and Straus, David, Wyden, NY, 1976 in *How To Make Meetings Work*.

In an effective interaction meeting each participant has a specific responsibility.

Responsibility of Chairman

This individual is an active participant in group process.
- ✓ Makes final decisions/sets constraints for meeting
- ✓ Establishes the agenda
- ✓ Speaks openly for his own point of view
- ✓ Deals with media and public in general
- ✓ Responsible for assignment of tasks and deadlines
- ✓ Represents the group in meetings with other groups

Responsibility of Facilitator

This person need *not* be the chairman. He is neutral servant of the group.
- ✓ Encourages participation from all attending
- ✓ Coordinates logistics of meeting
- ✓ Focuses attention of the group on a common task
- ✓ Refrains from evaluating ideas or participating in discussion
- ✓ Protects all ideas from attack
- ✓ Suggests alternate methods and procedures
- ✓ Helps the group find win/win solutions

Responsibility of Recorder

This person makes notes for use later by the secretary.
- ✓ Records and produces the Group Record (Minutes)
- ✓ Refrains from participating in discussion
- ✓ Writes down basic ideas with markers on large sheets in front of the participants
- ✓ Uses the speaker's words
- ✓ Makes note of "Action" items, with individuals responsible noted
- ✓ Frees ideas from the originator, unless his name is needed for a motion
- ✓ Provides a common focus for the group
- ✓ Posts sheets, as completed, for later review (particularly by those coming late)

Responsibility of Group Members

These are the participants in the meeting.
- ✓ Keeps the Recorder and Facilitator neutral
- ✓ Makes sure the information recorded is accurate
- ✓ Establishes "norms" for meeting
- ✓ Determines the course of the meeting. May make procedural suggestions; may overrule suggestions of the Facilitator
- ✓ Gives full attention to task of the meeting and to comments of fellow group members
- ✓ Keeps an open mind to new ideas and comments of others
- ✓ Avoids becoming defensive

Group Record   The Group Record is the running record of the meeting that allows the latecomer to see what has happened and what is going on now. As the minutes are recorded, no names are mentioned (except with assignment of tasks). These sheets are taped or pinned up where they can be seen by all. It permits the group to focus on the task at hand, rather than on each other.

"Action Items" are noted in another color next to the discussion item: i.e., "Check into possible meeting places big enough to accommodate 150 and available in mid-April. Carol T., by Oct. meeting."

Group Memo   The memo is what is usually called the *minutes*—instead, it is a typed copy of the Record. It divides the information into What Happened and How, and Decisions/Action Items. Highlight information specifically needed by an individual when mailing his copy to him. See Group memo form on facing page.

The major advantage in conducting an Interaction Meeting is the opportunity it provides for satisfaction by all attending. The objective is to establish consensus.

Consensus   Consensus is a win/win solution that everyone can accept. It's a solution that does not compromise any strong convictions or needs. It is not a compromise. You do not give up something to gain something else. It may not be what you feel is the ideal, but on the other hand you don't really feel you are losing anything important.

Essential considerations in an Interaction Meeting are:
Content — The **What** (problem, topic, agenda) and
Process — The **How** (approach, method, procedure).

If consensus cannot be reached, at least the group has made an effort and worked at collaboration. This experience is not lost. The members will have developed a real understanding of how much more productive the consensus approach is. It will become apparent that no one must lose in order for someone to win. Among the good things that come out of a consensus approach is the awareness each participant comes to that he is being *heard*, that his stand is being given a chance, that each option is being weighed objectively against an agreed-upon criteria for success.

MINUTES   I endorse Interaction Recording and the concepts outlined by Doyle
Interaction   and Straus (see Suggested Reading). Most committees and Boards
Recording   could increase their efficiency as well as the understanding of the members if they saved minutes for meetings larger than 30 and adopted the interactive approach to recording for smaller group meetings.

GROUP MEMO (MINUTES)

Committee Name: _____

Date of Meeting: _____

Place: _____

Team-Building Exercise: _____

Members Attending:_____

_____

_____

What Happened and How:

- _____

- _____

- _____

- _____

- _____

Decision Action Items: _____

Future Plans (Next Step):• _____

• _____

_____
(RECORDER)

With questions call: _____ Phone _____

© 1994 Emily Kittle Morrison, *Leadership Skills*, Fisher Books, Tucson, Arizona

Key points   For those situations where minutes are essential, such as large general meetings, here are some key points to remember:

- ❖ At the beginning, identify the group or committee, the kind of meeting, date, time and place
  - ✓ Identify chairman and secretary
  - ✓ List those in attendance and state that a quorum was present
  - ✓ Acknowledge the acceptance of previous minutes
  - ✓ Give financial report as previous balance, total receipts, disbursements and present balance only (full report may be attached)
  - ✓ Record all points of order and appeals for decision by the chair, whether lost or carried; secondary motions only when carried
  - ✓ Note points of discussion when instructed to by the group
  - ✓ Note that specific committee reports were given, cite key points only
  - ✓ Separate subjects by paragraphs
  - ✓ Identify any special speaker and the topic without further notation
  - ✓ Cite actual count for or against in recording votes
  - ✓ Identify each individual making a motion (those seconding need not be mentioned in the final draft)
  - ✓ Close with the time of adjournment and sign the sheet. "Respectfully submitted" is outdated, as is the phrase, "turn over" the meeting or podium.

Minutes should be kept in a notebook, preceded by those of the previous year. A copy of the minutes should always be sent to the Executive Committee.

To serve as an efficient and effective secretary in the traditional manner, the individual should take careful notes. From these he or she will be expected to compile minutes. The material must be accurate, precise, impartial and specific. The final minutes should be typed (or entered into a word-processor) and copies distributed within one week of the meeting. The president and committee chairmen should always receive a copy. When deemed necessary, the committee as a whole should also receive a copy.

Minutes that are mailed in advance need not be read for approval at the following meeting, though corrections should be noted. When indicated in the record that an attachment will be included, it should be sent with the minutes.

Minutes should record what was done, *not what was said*. They should also include all motions, including amendments. in exact wording (whether they passed or not) and who proposed them. These should be <u>underlined</u>. Motions that are adopted should be capitalized and appear with an asterisk in the left margin.

Minutes should *not* contain personal opinions or interpretations by the secretary, nor should they include descriptive phrases. Avoid adjectives and adverbs and concentrate on factual notes. Praise or criticism of members should appear only in the form of officially adopted notes of gratitude or commendation.

CHECKLIST FOR COMMITTEE CHAIRMEN

Every new chairman should carefully consider the many aspects of committee responsibility. The following is a useful tool for chairmen. An adaptation of this form might be included on Board orientation materials.

Committee Objectives

✤ Are the committee's (group's) objectives clearly stated and agreed upon by all?

✤ Are they realistic and pertinent to the purpose of the committee?

✤ Is it understood *who* is responsible for each objective and when it is to have been accomplished?

Committee Members

✤ Do they fully understand the function of the committee? Have you provided adequate orientation?

✤ Have you arranged for special training?

✤ Are they capable and motivated to carry out their assignments?

✤ Do you need a liaison member from a related committee to ensure continuity?

✤ Are you on the lookout for potential leaders?

Committee Meetings

✤ Have the goals, date and time of each meeting been agreed upon (to meet the schedules of the members)?

✤ Have you set a routine for meetings and scheduled each meeting well in advance?

✤ Have you selected a secretary, or do you plan to rotate the job of recorder?

✤ When additional people are needed, is it understood who will invite them?

✤ Do you report regularly from the Board to the committee and back to the Board?

✤ Are you cognizant of policies and bylaws applicable to your committee?

Committee Resources

✤ Do you have all the needed tools to function effectively?
  - ✓ Past reports
  - ✓ List of the organization's goals and objectives
  - ✓ A list of committee goals and objectives
  - ✓ Minutes of previous meetings
  - ✓ A Board manual (where applicable)
  - ✓ A copy of current bylaws

Committee Reports

✛ Do you have concise reports for regular Board meetings?

✛ How do you keep the group as a whole informed?
- ✓ Organization reports
- ✓ Newsletter articles
- ✓ Direct mailings
- ✓ Area meetings

✛ Have you prepared an annual report that includes:
- ✓ Stated goals and objectives
- ✓ Accomplishments

Committee Evaluation

✛ Have you scheduled an evaluation meeting?

✛ How do you propose to evaluate?
- ✓ Individual accomplishments
- ✓ Fulfillment of committee objectives
- ✓ Year's progress

✛ Have you established objectives and spelled out recommendations for next year's committee?

A CHAIRMAN'S GUIDE FOR CLIMATE SETTING

The following are key points for consideration before convening a meeting. Demonstrate an awareness of the positive nature of each point.

✛ People relate to each other more quickly in small groups.

✛ Exercises in sharing should be planned with the specific group in mind.

✛ Early questions should call for memories or experience readily available for everyone rather than opinions or ideas.

✛ The leader should demonstrate what he or she is asking others to do.

✛ It is important to allow for individual differences.

✛ The Chairman sets the stage. The attitude should be open and positive.

HOW TO HANDLE TYPICAL PROBLEMS

Problems with meetings can be greatly diminished by efforts suggested earlier in this chapter. However, should you face any of the common frustrations associated with meetings, the following points are intended as helpful suggestions.

Late-comers

✛ Make sure extra seating is closest to the door, near needed handouts

✛ Post the "Group Memory" (see Interaction Recording)

✛ Always start on time—few people will show up late

✛ Don't make an issue of their tardiness but involve latecomers at the first opportunity

Committee Reports	✤ Try using a Board Packet (print minutes and treasurer's report at beginning, following the agenda)
	✤ Allow just 2 minutes for reporting committee chairmen
	✤ Use visual aids or skits for variety
	✤ Use a brief, standard "news release" form (see Publicity)
Lengthy Speakers	✤ Clarify the time allotted up front
	✤ Notify speaker when there are 5 minutes left
	✤ Help the speaker to start on time
	✤ Sit near the speaker so you can tactfully cut him off
A Famous Guest in Your Midst	✤ Arrange some informal time in advance of the meeting
	✤ Put him or her at the beginning of your program
	✤ Provide a question-answer time
	✤ Provide the person with information about your group
Decide on a Resource Person	✤ Observe the person in another setting
	✤ Review your needs with him in advance, by phone or in person
	✤ Consider the evaluation of respected members who know him
Assurance that Arrangements Will be as Requested	✤ Visit the site in advance, speak directly with those in charge
	✤ Request a floor plan and map out your needs on several copies
	✤ Commit one member to be responsible for arrangements
	✤ Have a walk-through of your activities (at least mentally)
	✤ Arrive early enough to deal with misunderstandings or changes
	✤ Send a copy of your objectives and plans to all concerned
Apathy Among Members	✤ Divide into small groups to identify the nature of the problem
	✤ Hold a structured discussion to isolate why members feel there is apathy
	✤ Allow a scheduled time to break into buzz groups to consider the issue
	✤ Consider using a group assessment survey that allows for anonymous responses
Participants Who Come Unprepared	✤ Brainstorm for ideas to solve the identified problem
	✤ Be sure your agenda spells out preparation needed
	✤ Set a good example
	✤ Openly discuss the problem created and appeal to the group for suggestions

❖ On the agenda, run a yellow highlighter over the individual's assignment to call attention to it

❖ Always have specified deadlines

❖ Follow through. Let participants know what you expect of them

❖ Build on the positive; avoid dwelling on the negative

❖ Move on

❖ Learn to delegate to responsible associates (see Delegation)

EXERCISES—TO BUILD A SENSE OF TEAM

❖ **First Meeting**

For 1 or 2 minutes, ask everyone to guess the biography of one of the members. Family, skills, hobbies, employment, experiences, abilities, etc. At the end of the guessing, that person will tell how close the guess has come to the truth. The next person then becomes the focus. Repeat the process.

Offer a forced preference of choices to the group. Each member is asked to select the one which most closely suits his outlook and move to one part of the room or the other. Each smaller group is then asked to discuss individually the reasons for choosing that group. The process is repeated, with new choices, and regrouping for 5 or 6 options.

The following are some possible suggestions:

✓ I like to be seen as *efficient* or *friendly.*

✓ I would rather be a *chairman* or a *group member.*

✓ I prefer *making decisions on my own* or *with a group.*

✓ *I tend to be happier working with a group or working alone.*

❖ **For Learning More About Old Colleagues**

✓ Have each group member fill out a 3 x 5 card in pencil with 2 "truths" and 1 "lie."

✓ Shuffle the cards and one by one read the cards, allowing all members to guess who each card represents. Read all first, then go back—coding them—1-2-3, etc.

✓ Acknowledge which card is yours and then let the members attempt to select the "lie."

✓ Share and clarify.

Personal Lifeline

❖ Arrange members in subgroups of 4 or 5.

❖ Ask each member to draw his lifeline with its up's and down's, highlights and disappointments, from the time he can remember to the present. Code each change of direction.

❖ Ask members of each sub-group to explain their lifelines to one another.

❖ Ask the members if they can discover any common threads in their experiences.

Mingle Sharing

1. Ask each member to write three things about themselves, each on separate cards.

2. Place the cards in a basket and have each member select three (not their own).

3. Participants are then to find the individuals who filled out the cards they drew.

4. When everyone has been identified the group sits down and each person takes turn giving his name. This is followed by the people with his cards each adding what they learned about him.

If you come out of your meetings wondering "What happened?" maybe it is time for you to become more involved, to take up the banner of Bear Bryant: *"Cause something to happen!"* If you are in charge, decide what needs to happen and set about to accomplish this.

If you are simply a frustrated member, then speak to someone in charge. Describe your observations and express your concerns about the possible consequences. If the listener is receptive, propose possible non-threatening positive solutions. But . . . cause *something* to happen!. Not to decide is to decide!. If *nothing* constructive is done, *something* negative will probably happen.

Everybody knows that there are three 'bodies" in every group: *Somebody, Anybody,* and *Nobody.* 'When the Chairman asked for volunteers he said, *"Anybody* can do it." *Everybody* thought *Somebody* would, but *Nobody* did.

The *Somebody* decided that since *Anybody* could but *Nobody* did, then *Somebody* should and so he volunteered.

When *Everybody* saw *Somebody* doing what *Anybody* could, *everybody* gladly lent a hand . . and soon the job was done!!!

YOU DO MAKX A DIFFXRXNCX

Xvxn though my typxwritrxr is an old modxl, it rxally works quitx wxll; that is xxcxpt onx kxy. I havx ofttxn wishxd that it workxd pxrfxctly. It is trux that thxrx arx 41 othxr kxys that do function wxll xnough . . . but just onx not working makxs a diffrxncx.

Next time you think, "I'm only one person, my vote (or opinion) won't count"— remember, you do make a difference, and there is much in it for you if you'll speak up and contribute. You can't win the sweepstakes unless you enter.

RATE YOUR MEETING

Whether a leader or participant, you can determine how well your meeting works by evaluating the following "dimensions." After each item, circle the number that most accurately describes that dimension of your meeting

1 This is a problem area for us.
2 We do "okay" with this, but could definitely improve.
3 This is one of our strengths.

The higher your total, the more likely you already are having effective, productive meetings. The lower your score, the more likely you will want to read on and begin to apply some of the ideas presented here.

Making Decisions

Making decisions in a way that ensures both quality work and acceptance by participants is essential if a meeting is to be effective. Each of us wants to feel that we influence the decisions made in meetings we attend. The more closely a decision reflects a consensus of the group, the stronger the support and the commitment on the part of individual participants.

1 2 3

Working Together

A group that works well together in meetings focuses on the task or agenda at hand and works to maintain adequate trust, involvement and support among its members. To function effectively a group must take care of its people as well as its agenda.

1 2 3

Organization and Procedures

Groups that meet successfully have a clearly understood organization and procedures so participants know what to expect in terms of their groups' operation. But it is essential that the organization and procedures be flexible enough to deal with changing situations and information.

1 2 3

Goals

The goals for meetings are clearly understood and accepted by individual participants. What is to be accomplished in each meeting is clearly established, and the overall goals and purpose for the meetings are identified and articulated for the entire group.

1 2 3

Participant Resources

An effective group makes the best possible use of the ideas, suggestions, and strengths of individual participants. Their contributions will be invited and encouraged by the way the meeting is conducted. Members feel as if they are an essential part of the meeting process—which they are!

1 2 3

Communication

Groups that work well together maintain effective communication between both individuals and subgroups. Effective communication includes careful listening and thoughtful, clear self-expression. It means shared responsibility for being sure that information and meaning are exchanged fully and with understanding.

1 2 3

Leadership

Leadership in meetings that work is a shared responsibility. The person who is the designated leader recognizes and carries out his or her tasks. Individual participants look to themselves as contributing to the *leadership* of the meeting.

1 2 3

Conflicts, Disagreements, Feelings

Effective groups regard conflict or disagreement and the expression of feeling as an opportunity to improve the meeting rather than something to be avoided. As a result, the meeting will be handled constructively to clarify positions or feelings so these become new information available to the group as it works.

1 2 3

Process

In effective meetings, participants are aware of and and pay attention to process, because it is an ongoing source of how well they are working together. This means paying attention to their immediate experience in meetings, and periodically evaluating the effectiveness of their meetings in "process" terms.

1 2 3

© 1994 Emily Kittle Morrison, *Leadership Skills*, Fisher Books, Tucson, Arizona

3

Board Skills

"How to Build a Better Board"

Volunteer organizations are formed in response to many social needs. They may be established to offer social services, cultural or recreational programs, educational resources or simply a "sense of belonging."

A Board of Directors has responsibility for the organization's operation, for stability and for continuity. Community Boards can mean the difference between public understanding and support of volunteer efforts, and public apathy. Boards that understand their role and fulfill their responsibilities effectively can make a significant difference in a community.

Volunteers provide a quality of insight and caring that cannot be replaced by theoretical expertise or legislated services. The volunteer who feels needed and valued as a Board member will experience personal growth and continue to be concerned and involved in the organization or agency.

BOARD MEMBERS Individuals who indicate a willingness to serve as Board members should do so with full awareness of the obligations that accompany the position. In some situations the position implies simply dealing with policies and decisions that affect the organization. However, just as often the position results from the fact that you are a committee chairman and are responsible for a particular project or activity for the group.

When the latter is the case, keep in mind that you will be wearing two hats. You will primarily focus your attention on executing the tasks related to your committee assignment, including the responsibility to report your progress to the Board. But you also need to give your attention to the activities of the Board as a whole, to weigh the issues presented by other chairmen. You can bring a needed perspective, a new *objective* one, to the proposals of others. Be prepared to exercise the obligation to listen and to respond. The effectiveness of the Board's decisions depends on this.

Before you can expect volunteers to join in your cause or support your organization, you must clarify your purpose. Why do you exist? What do you hope to accomplish? What is your reason for being?

CLARIFYING YOUR PURPOSE

Ten questions to ask when formulating a Mission Statement:*

1. Why do we exist?

2. What business are we in?

3. What is our most important product/service?

4. Who are our clients? . . . volunteers? . . donors?

5. Why do they come to us?

6. How have we changed in the last five years?

7. What are our unique strengths?

8. What are our major weaknesses?

9. What philosophical issues are most important to us?

10. What would be lost if we ceased to exist?

DUTIES OF A BOARD MEMBER

Individuals who agree to serve on a Board should do so with the understanding that there are duties that accompany this position. The Nominating Committee needs to have reason to believe each potential Board Member recognizes these obligations and understands the duties.

❖ To exercise power for the benefit of the organization and all of its members with full honesty and reasonable efficiency

❖ To exercise greatest care, skill and judgment

❖ To act out of good faith and deal fairly with the organization

❖ To display highest loyalty, reasonable care and business prudence in regard to the interests of the organization

*Based on material by the Public Management Institute

Diligence   Board Members are expected to perform with diligence. This implies that Board Members should:

❖ be fully aware of the duties and obligations of their positions.

❖ be able to devote the time necessary to fulfill their responsibilities.

❖ actively take part in the Board's decision-making process.

❖ actively oversee the action of their organization.

❖ scrutinize the official records and financial statements of their organization and question subordinates about them in a way that would be deemed reasonable.

Prudence   Prudence involves the avoidance of acts demonstrating lack of loyalty or good faith. With regard to loyalty, a Board member's primary concern must be avoidance of conflicts of interest.

Board members can be held liable. A board position should be taken seriously. Under the law, yours is more than a name on a letterhead. (see page 35 and the appendix for additional information).

When developing a job description for the key positions on your Board, the following guidelines should be considered and expanded. Beyond the general points made, a job description should specify those activities that relate particularly to the Board in question. This should be done because there will be differences. Conflict, confusion and duplication of effort can be forestalled by a clear job description.

RESPONSIBILITIES OF ORGANIZATION MEMBERS
Executive Director

❖ Serve as chief of operations for the organization

❖ Act as professional advisor to the Board

❖ Recommend appropriate policies for consideration

❖ Effectively implement all policies adopted by the Board

❖ Fully and accurately inform the Board with regard to programs

❖ Interpret the needs of programs and present recommendations on all problems and issues faced by the Board

❖ Develop a budget with the finance committee and keep the Board posted on the budget situation

❖ Recruit the best personnel, develop a competent staff and supervise effectively

❖ Develop and improve the staff

❖ Assist the Board in developing and conducting community information and education

Board of Directors
- Counsel and advise, sharing benefit of judgment, expertise and familiarity
- Consult with the Executive Director on all matters to be considered by the Board
- Delegate responsibility for all Executive functions
- Hold the staff responsible to the Executive Director
- Share all communications with the Executive Director
- Provide support to the Executive Director and staff in carrying out professional duties
- Support the Executive Director in all decisions and actions consistent with policies and standards of the organization
- Hold the Executive Director accountable for supervision
- Help develop operating funds
- Evaluate the work of the Executive Director annually
- Perform in a prudent and diligent manner

Board President
- Provide leadership in expediting goals of the organization
- Guide the Board in fulfilling its stated roles
- Facilitate meetings to assure adequate discussion in an organized manner
- Invest the Board's time wisely
- Represent the Board in supervising the Executive Director
- Supervise the chairmen of standing committees
- Represent the organization in matters that affect it
- Develop the leadership potential of Board members
- Enhance the organization's image in the community
- Perform as an admirable role model for other volunteers
- Offer continuing praise and appreciation to Board members

SELECTING NEW BOARD MEMBERS

A Board might ask itself the following questions before looking for new members:

✓ What do we need? (people with specific expertise, a fund-raiser, money, influential names, minorities, workers, etc.)

✓ What do we expect? (spell it out—time, financial obligations, meeting attendance, committee work, etc.)

✓ Where are we going? Can the person help us get there?

✓ Why are we doing this? Will it make sense to this person?

A prospective Board member might ask himself and the Board the following questions before making a commitment to serve:

✓ What is expected of me?

✓ What is the organization's purpose? The Board's purpose? Do I believe in it?

✓ What am I going to get out of this?

✓ Is this the challenge I'm looking for?

✓ Do I have the time?

✓ Do I have the expertise?

✓ Am I comfortable with this group?

An effective Board enlists the collective wisdom of carefully selected members. Each member brings unique knowledge, insight, skill and personal contacts. By working together a *synergism* takes effect. Separate ideas blend together to build a whole greater than the parts. In weighing alternatives, collective judgment brings a community perspective to issues at hand.

An effective Board interprets programs and builds support for the mission of the organization. Board members act as liaisons with the broad base of the community while providing continuity for purpose and policy.

LIABILITIES OF A BOARD*

When an individual agrees to sit on a Board he becomes a part of a group that may provide great camaraderie, a chance to make a difference in the community for a cause he cares about and a challenge to his skills. But Board participation also involves certain liabilities that each new member should consider carefully before accepting a position.

You have a responsibility to:

✤ Attend Board and committee meetings regularly.

✤ Be familiar with the minutes of the Board and committee to which you are assigned.

*Based on material from the Institute for Voluntary Organizations

❖ Be familiar with your organization's publications.

❖ Treat the affairs of the organization as you would your own.

❖ Be certain your organization's records are audited by a reputable CPA firm, that tax returns are prepared and submitted on a timely basis to the state and federal authorities (IRS etc.)

❖ Be familiar with your organization's goals, objectives and programs.

❖ Insist that all committee meetings are reported to the Board.

❖ Know your organization's budget, budget process and financial situation, as well as that of any committee to which you are assigned.

❖ Know who is authorized to sign checks and in what amount.

❖ Avoid self-serving policies.

❖ If there is something you do not understand or comes to your attention that causes you to question a policy or practice, ask for advice.

❖ Insist that there is a well-established personnel program with a competent staff chief executive.

❖ Avoid the substance or appearance of conflict of interest.

❖ Be certain your organization is fulfilling all aspects of its not-for-profit and tax-exempt status.

❖ Insist on a written nominating procedure.

❖ Monitor the community and professional image of your organization.

❖ Be certain the policies are clearly identified and that the board acts on them as a whole rather than by action of a small group of individuals.

❖ Know your organization: Board of Directors, financial condition, programs and staff before you accept membership.

❖ Require that your organization have proper legal counsel

❖ Monitor the activities of your executive committee to ensure it does not overstep its authority.

❖ Insist that the Board have a policy with regard to volunteer liability (including Board members).

❖ See Appendix for additional material

Be fully aware of the duties and obligations of membership before agreeing to sit on a Board. Request a clear job description. Take an active part in the decision-making process, even when the issue isn't one which personally affects you. Develop the "people skills" necessary to implement what you know to be good and just. **How** you do what you choose to do ultimately determines the success you experience in **what** you do.

CONSIDERATIONS FOR A BALANCED BOARD																												
RELATIONSHIPS	Access to community leaders, groups																											
	Access to neighborhood leaders, groups																											
	Access to people with expertise																											
	Access to people with money																											
GEOGRAPHIC AREA REPRESENTED	County (name)																											
	County (name)																											
	City (name)																											
	City (name)																											
	At Large																											
	Immediate neighborhood																											
AREA OF EXPERTISE	Public Relations																											
	Financial Management																											
	Fundraising																											
	Personnel Administration																											
	Legal																											
	Evaluation																											
	Program																											
SANCTION	Medical																											
	Small Business																											
	Local Media																											
	Churches																											
	Corporate																											
	Political																											
	Education																											
	Law Enforcement																											
	Neighborhood																											
	Union																											
RACE OR ETHINC REPRESENTATION	Caucasian																											
	Native American																											
	Black																											
	Hispanic																											
	Asian																											
	Other																											
AGE	Over 65																											
	51 - 65																											
	36 - 50																											
	20 - 35																											
SEX	Female																											
	Male																											
BOARD COMPOSITION ANALYSIS	YEARS ON BOARD																											
	BOARD MEMBERS																											
	TERMS TO CONTINUE																				**TERMS EXPIRE ---**							

© 1994 Emily Kittle Morrison, *Leadership Skills*, Fisher Books, Tucson, Arizona

TYPICAL BOARD PROBLEMS

Most problems that develop within Boards stem from one of the five following areas. By identifying those that seem to face your group you are then in a position to begin to resolve the problem. Look at the list and consider what you might do to alleviate the situation, once you have isolated the problem. For example, if Board members seem unsure of the dimensions of their jobs it is time to begin to develop job descriptions for each position.

❖ **Fear**
  ✓ Of looking inept to others
  ✓ Of what others might think
  ✓ Of not really being up to the job
  ✓ Of asking questions and appearing inexperienced
  ✓ Of expressing opinions that might differ
  ✓ Of the others, because of who they are

❖ **Lack of Skills**
  ✓ In working with others as a group
  ✓ In organization, administration and planning
  ✓ In decision-making and problem-solving
  ✓ In research and development
  ✓ In being an effective participant in a meeting

❖ **Lack of information as to:**
  ✓ Dimensions of their job
  ✓ Lines and extent of authority
  ✓ Their specific roles
  ✓ Their responsibility and accountability
  ✓ Not knowing they don't know

❖ **Lack of leadership**
  ✓ Serving under an unskilled Director
  ✓ No preparation for the specific responsibilities
  ✓ Presided over by an ill-equipped president

❖ **Lack of understanding as to purpose**
  ✓ Feeling Boards are rubber stamps and are there only for social reasons
  ✓ Failure to conduct an annual Board Orientation
  ✓ Failure to identify needs and resources of members
  ✓ Inability to recognize how they fit with the the agency

All too often money is not allocated for Board training, nor is time. Even experienced Board members need time to build a sense of team in a new group, with new people and new challenges. Board members need structured time in which to build a sense of trust, to develop pertinent skills, and to assess needs and opportunities. Board Orientation and Board Training should be annual events, at least.

BOARD ORIENTATION SESSION

The following is presented as a guide for developing a Board Orientation session. It is a checklist of things to consider including:

When:_____ Individual Responsible: _____

ASSESSMENT OF NEEDS OF INCOMING BOARD MEMBERS
(IN TERMS OF SKILLS AND SPECIFIC KNOWLEDGE)
- ✓ As individuals
- ✓ As a functioning chairman
- ✓ As an effective Board member
- ✓ As a good communicator
- ✓ As a member of the team. What strengths do they bring to their positions?

Knowledge the executive commitee should have in advance of orientation

INFORMATION ON HOW BOARDS WORK
- ✓ Existing jobs and responsibilities of each member
- ✓ Relationships that exist (which committees work together, who should report to whom, etc.)
- ✓ How individuals and committees communicate within the structure (Publicity guidelines, inter-organizational communication, liaisons, etc.)
- ✓ How decisions are made, policies set, planning accomplished
- ✓ Current Board and committee objectives and their inter-relationship

Material that should be provided in a Board Orientation packet

BOARD RESPONSIBILITIES/COMMITTEE RESPONSIBILITIES
(AND A ROSTER OF BOARD MEMBERS)

Outlines that should be included in the Board Orientation packet

BUILDING A SENSE OF TEAM, OF CONFIDENCE, OF SELF-WORTH

Involve members in an activity and review the reasons for their ongoing concern for their committee members

INFORMATION ON
- ✓ Group process
- ✓ Situational leadership
- ✓ Roles of a Board member
- ✓ Communication/Motivation
- ✓ Decision-making
- ✓ Problem-Solving
- ✓ Conflict management

Either as resource material or by way of active involvement in concepts with a visual presentation of ideas such as exercises conducted by a trainer

HOW TO MAKE MEETINGS WORK
- ✓ Interaction Meeting explanation
- ✓ Consent agendas and how to structure an agenda
- ✓ Group memo and minutes
- ✓ Your first meeting as a Chairman (purpose, duties, interrelationships, responsibilities, history, on-going activities, policies and procedures, objectives and a review of expectations —yours and theirs)

An explanation and review of these concepts

PARLIAMENTARY PROCEDURE AT A GLANCE

Resource material

INFORMATION AT A GLANCE/ REVIEW OF BOARD MANUAL

Resource materials

OFFICE PROCEDURES

Resource material

FINANCIAL PROCEDURES

Resource material

© 1994 Emily Kittle Morrison, *Leadership Skills*, Fisher Books, Tucson, Arizona

BOARD ORIENTATION

A Board Orientation gets members functioning faster as a team. It clarifies levels of authority and expectations. It allows members to begin to feel a part of the group. And it provides individuals with tools for effectiveness.

A Board orientation should be held annually when new officers are elected. This formality assures a sense of belonging and understanding. It gives each member an opportunity to develop a sense of team and to understand assignments, policies and expectations. It should begin with an Icebreaker appropriate to the makeup of the group (see page 48).

When a Board meets it has a chance to feel and see itself truly as a group. This happens only when members gather in the same room to work on the same task. How the individual members feel about the group, how much they feel like a part of the team and how committed they are will depend on what effort has been made to develop camaraderie among the members.

Step 1

A review of your mission statement could be considered as one of the first activities in any orientation. There is often a discrepancy between members as to the exact purpose of both the organization and the Board. For this reason it is important to establish agreement among the Board members early in their association.

Step 2

A second step in this process is to identify the focus areas, which may be identified as committees. Perhaps some committees were formed decades ago and no longer serve a useful purpose. On the other hand, you may discover the need for a committee that has never been set up, but that would help facilitate the current mission and established goals.

Committee Ideas

At this point Board members could generate ideas as to:

✤ The purpose and goal of the committee (Description)

✤ Realistic objectives that are measurable

✤ Factors working in your favor for successful achievement of these objectives, and

✤ Obstacles that should be anticipated and may have to be overcome

✤ The money, manpower and time needed to achieve the identified objectives

✤ The skills needed to succeed on this committee

✤ The skills to be acquired through participation on this committee

✤ The training that might be needed

✤ And, the line of authority for decisions

The following form should be filled out before recruiting anyone to a position on the Board. People recruited for their specific skills, interests and abilities (aligned with the "tasks this person must do") are ultimately the most valuable Board members. To recruit effectively, invest time in clarifying your expectations for the person. Only approach qualified people!

© 1994 Emily Kittle Morrison, *Leadership Skills*, Fisher Books, Tucson, Arizona

JOB CLARIFICATION

Position: _____

TASKS PERFORMED ON THE JOB	TO DO THIS TASK A PERSON MUST		
	KNOW ABOUT	BE ABLE TO	BELIEVE OR FEEL THAT

TIME COMMITMENT: (Length of Board term)	MONETARY COMMITMENT: (Board dues)

For any Board member to succeed as a committee chairman a well-defined job description is needed. Much time is lost, confusion created and unnecessary conflict developed simply because there was no clear understanding on the part of Board members and their president as to what was expected of the other.

Integrating New Board Members

Ideas for integration onto a new Board include:

❖ Assign a sponsor to look after new members, make introductions, answer questions.

❖ Arrange for informal social time, either in conjunction with Board meetings or by special arrangement.

❖ Lead a tour of the agency or organization's office to acquaint the individual with the facility and the staff.

❖ Prepare a packet explaining the mission/purpose, policies, programs, committees, bylaws, budget, personnel and expectations, along with an organizational chart.

❖ Give the new member a specific job to do! When he has a chance to make a contribution he becomes personally involved.

❖ Offer skill training to alleviate any apprehension about doing the job.

BOARD AND STAFF ORIENTATION
Responsibilities

Far too often staff members are uncertain as to how to work with Board members and frequently Board members do not have a clear understanding of how to work with staff. Time should be allocated to discuss these issues together.

❖ Relationships should be understood. A balance should be created for viability and consistency. Include an organizational chart.

❖ Expectations of each should be identified and fully clarified. Who determines policy, administers operations, plans program delivery, delivers program, recruits new Board members, establishes salary, evaluates organization results, assesses problems, approves budget?

❖ Areas of responsibility should be included in a Board manual

Team Work

❖ Job descriptions should be developed, including skills needed and skills gained

❖ Principles of the partnership should be discussed and nurtured.
  ✓ Honest, open communication
  ✓ Atmosphere of mutual confidence
  ✓ Identification and agreement on the mission of the organization
  ✓ Clarification of responsibilities

✤ Communications should be encouraged.
  ✓ Reason for working together understood: To augment,
    not aggravate
  ✓ Clarification of interdependence
  ✓ Commit members to a group process and develop an
    interactive approach
  ✓ Acknowledge that they are accountable as a unit
  ✓ Develop an understanding of roles and develop a line
    of authority

BOARD MANUAL   A Board Manual is a notebook that provides the Board member with an easy resource for understanding and clarification. It should be distributed at Board Orientation.

Checklist for   ✤ Organization's purpose statement
Board Manual
         ✤ Constitution and by-laws

         ✤ Organization goals and current plans

         ✤ Annual report

         ✤ Budget and financial report

         ✤ Program description/goals and objectives

         ✤ Organizational chart (staff names and numbers)

         ✤ Committees (standing or ad hoc) and their goals and plans

         ✤ Any evaluations conducted during past year

         ✤ Personnel roster

         ✤ Personnel policies and expectations

         ✤ Board list—with names, addresses and phone numbers

         ✤ Meeting information: days, dates, length of meetings, place

         ✤ Minutes from meetings for last fiscal year

         ✤ Any appropriate procedures governing conduct of meetings

BOARD   A Board packet is a collection of pertinent material that is distributed in
PACKET   advance of a Board meeting. It allows members to come prepared and
         to communicate their intent more accurately.

What It Is   ✤ A communiqué that brings Board members up to date on
         committees' actions since the last meeting.

         ✤ It includes each committee chairman's report, minutes and financial
           reports as well as items that will come to a vote.

What It Does
- Saves time—Minutes, Corresponding Secretary and Treasurer's reports, special dates, announcements and information are printed and reviewed for questions or discussion instead of being read aloud. It brings the Board up to date and eliminates the need for committee chairman to report, unless they have an Action Item.

- Improves decision-making—The packet provides important background information on committee recommendations that will be discussed at the Board meeting. Board members who have read the packet materials are prepared for focused and intelligent discussion and action.

How it Works
Board members request that information pertinent to their reports be included in the agenda. Example: If a motion is to be presented, the motion should be stated with any background necessary information on a sheet in the Board packet.

- The agenda for the meeting is included in the packet. The agenda can be divided into two parts:
  - ✓ Consent Agenda items include items that require no discussion or decision. Items such as correspondence listing, announcements from committee Chair and the Treasurer's report could be included. A Board member may request that an item on the Consent Agenda be removed and placed on the Action Agenda.
  - ✓ Action Agenda items include: motions to be voted on, reports from Project Chairs, Ways and Means report, as well as additional old business and new business.

- An individual needs to be assigned to collect and assemble the information monthly, as well as to distribute it to each Board member. This can be mailed or it can be the responsibility of each Board member to pick up his or hers at a designated time and place.

What You Do
- Anticipate Board meetings—Plan your committee meetings so that recommendations or anything requiring Board action make the deadline set in the packet sent in advance of the meeting.

- Come to the Board with solutions or proposals not problems. Include brief background and summary of pros and cons. Write out motions.

- Type your material. Put the name of committee, chairman, your phone number and date at top of page. Outline form is fine. Be brief.

- Deliver material to Secretary, or person assigned, 10 days prior to Board meeting.

- Distribute compiled packet a few days before Board meeting.

Meetings are thus expedited. Many items put in writing serve not only as a reminder to members, but assure accuracy of information. This packet should be kept in an ongoing Board notebook (manual).

TEAM BUILDING Individual needs, group needs and *task needs* are all present during any group interaction. A Board can't work as a team if they don't feel like a team. Personal needs are strongest in the beginning, and because of this, until they are met the group never really moves on.

Members should be helped to become *oriented* to the personalities within the group and the expectations of the group. After this takes place, each is better able to answer whether his personal needs will be met in this group.

Until Board members have a chance to to develop a sense of team, nothing can really be accomplished successfully. If members come time and time again and never seem to know where the group is coming from, where it is going, or how they fit into the scheme, then they will experience frustration. This frustration will prevent members from concentrating on the group needs and they will be unable to make a meaningful contribution.

Task and Process The *task* needs are the surface needs that bring people together in the first place. But it is difficult to focus on these objectives if there is conflict on the more basic level, involving *the process.*

Team-building exercises can help to assure that groups work together with a common focus. Even if the members know one another, there is no guarantee that for any one project they will truly feel like a team. Investing time at the beginning of each meeting for a team-building exercise will reap substantial rewards in the long run. These need not be "cutesy" or too involved.

Team-building exercises are most practical for committees or groups of fewer than 30. They differ from "icebreakers" in that icebreakers are designed to introduce new members and set them at ease. Team Builders help people get to know one another better. If the people working together on a task do not feel like a team, they won't perform like a team.

On the other hand, once you develop a team feeling within the group, tension is reduced and support for one another is generated. Members begin to see how their responsibilities are integrated with and dependent on the success of the activities of the rest of the group. Frustration with co-workers diminishes as members become more open to sharing success and concerns with one another. They also develop an understanding of the obstacles the others are facing.

The following represents a sampling of ideas for team building. I encourage you to adapt each to your group and to build into the exercises meaningful ideas or concepts. For example, if you are the core committee for the art auction, in the Forced Choice exercise you might ask them to divide by—a Picasso or a Rembrandt; a Calder or a Remington. If you're working on the Follies: a modern dancer or a soloist; an emcee or a comedian.

Use your imagination and at all times be aware of the willingness of your group to devote time to such activities. If you introduce the idea on a positive note and periodically demonstrate how it has helped, as a result of having taken the time to build a team feeling, those involved will begin to look forward to these activities. New ones can be tried by assigning this responsibility to different members each meeting.

IDEAS FOR TEAM BUILDING

✤ Milling and matching

✤ Art/Graphic exercises

✤ Games—Contests

✤ Round Robins

✤ Sign Boards with information

✤ Recall exercises

✤ Treasure Hunt

✤ Resource Hunt

✤ Bingo for group characteristics

✤ Sentence completion

✤ Inventing with given objects

✤ Mini-role-play

✤ Group or individual art projects

✤ Private fantasy exercises

✤ Partner interview

✤ One-minute biography

✤ Group effort, collaboration

✤ Graffiti board and discussion

✤ Divide and discuss

Sample Exercises

1. Stand if you did any of the following over the summer (good for a first fall meeting of an existing committee or group). The chairman asks, how many . . . ?
   ✓ Left the country this year?
   ✓ Suffered a sunburn this summer?
   ✓ Had houseguests?
   ✓ Learned something new (like water skiing)?
   ✓ Got away alone with your spouse?

2. Divide into buzz groups of 5 or 6, or go around the room allowing each member to participate, if the group is small. Have members complete a sentence—briefly:
   ✓ As a volunteer my greatest strength is . . .
   ✓ I'm uncomfortable when . . .
   ✓ I usually try to make people think I'm . . .
   ✓ I'm really concerned about . . .
   ✓ I love working with people who . . .
   ✓ In this group I have felt . . .
   ✓ If I had it to do all over again, I'd . . .
   ✓ I wish I could . . .
   ✓ It concerns me that . . .

3. Provide each participant with two 8-1/2 x 11 sheets of heavy paper. On one each is asked to write something he feels comfortable doing and enjoys talking about; this he pins on his front. On the second sheet he is asked to put something he would like to know more about; this he pins on his back. The group then mingles during the coffee hour, using the sheets as vehicles for conversation.

4. Forced selection. With this exercise you line up the group in the middle of the room and ask them to go to the right for one choice or the left for the other.
   Do you see yourself as:

a leader	or	a follower
a luxury car	or	a compact car
a rose	or	a wildflower
a glass of soda	or	a glass of champagne
a designer outfit	or	a pair of jeans
a sunny day	or	a cozy evening

   After each selection the subgroups should talk among themselves about why they made the choice they did.

5. Paired sharing. Take turns sharing with a partner:
   ✓ Two things you like about yourself
   ✓ One skill you feel you have
   ✓ One of your most satisfying achievements

6. To break down role barriers, have each participant take a turn walking across the room from point A to point B. The catch is that each must take a different path. Save those members with the most intimidating positions for last (such as CEO's). Most of the formality will be dropped by the time the 30th person seeks to go yet *another* way.

7. When you want to form several subgroups, you could try giving each participant a paper with a song title on it. Everyone is asked to hum his or her melody and to locate the others in the room with the same tune. If you want four to a group, distribute four cards with the same song title or sound, five if you want five, etc.

8. A good exercise when a little ego-boosting is needed is one used effectively in groups that have worked together as a team for a while. The idea is to form a circle and focus on one person, each of the others make a positive statement about that individual. Repeat the exercise until all involved have been the recipient of praise. Or, if the group is too large, you can go around the room and tell something positive about the person on your right.

9. Another idea is to share with the group the last thing you did before coming to the meeting. It can be very revealing. Or, where

would you like to be if you could be anywhere? Or, tell me something about yourself I couldn't know if you didn't tell me.

10. A more difficult but revealing exercise is to have members pair up and share an experience with one another that the individual felt especially good about—a feeling of accomplishment or achievement.

Team-building exercises and icebreakers can be used effectively on the committee level, and with adaptation, with the group as a whole. Think creatively about what you might do to introduce ideas such as these into your organizational activities. The time invested in team building pays many rewards.

ICEBREAKERS

Icebreakers are generally distinguished from team builders in that they are to help a group of strangers feel comfortable with one another for a short duration—such as in a conference or training session. Team builders are designed to help "build a sense of team." The following are ideas for use with groups of people who will only be together for a brief time, but should be made to feel at ease.

Paired Introductions

Each person meets and gets to know one other person, and in turn introduces his partner to the entire group.

One-Minute Autobiography

Break into small groups (up to ten) and with a timekeeper, give each person one minute to tell about himself (not his job, family, town, hobbies— but attitudes and values).

Depth Unfolding Process

In small groups give each member five minutes—the first two to share with the others what brought you to this point in your life, one minute to tell of your life, one minute to tell of your happiest moment, and one to answer questions (leader goes first).

Press Release

Write a press release about yourself and read it to the group. An alternative is to interview someone else and write a press release on that person.

Life Map

Using a crayon, on newsprint, each person creates a picture of his or her life (with stick figures and symbols).

Name Circle

Go around the circle saying your name and then repeating the names of all who have preceded you. An alternative is to state your name and explain how you got it.

Personalized Name Tags Let members create their own name tags. Provide: pens, 3 x 5 cards, old magazines, scissors and glue. Once created, they are asked to mingle and share with others why they chose the pictures they did.

Free Vacation Give everyone a 3 x 5 card and ask them to write where they'd rather be than here. Share.

Yarn Ball Give everyone a length of yarn (these should be of varying lengths). Ask that they tell the group about themselves, talking for as long as it takes to wrap the yarn around a finger.

Pocket or Purse Each participant takes any object from their purse or pocket and explains to the group what it says about them.

Graffitti Board Have participants draw and write on butcher paper stretched across one wall. Each should create something that reveals who he or she is in the context of this group. Use colorful pens or markers.

Active Image Each person is asked to state his or her name and give the others a line about how they can remember it. "My name is Barbara Byrd—and I fly south in the winter."

"I Am" In this exercise participants are given an 8½ X 11-inch sheet of paper on which they write six statements about who they are. "I am Sue Smythe,
  ✓ an engineer
  ✓ a new resident
  ✓ a fun-loving person
  ✓ a gardener
  ✓ a chocoholic
  ✓ a first-generation American"

Taking turns, each participant then shows the group their list and reads each point to the members.

Anytime a group of people is being asked to spend some time together in a group or in training they will feel more comfortable if they can get to know at least a few others in the room. It can only take place if there is a facilitated activity. *Not* everyone is outgoing enough to meet new people without such things as icebreakers.

"I Am a Resource" Ask each member to give their name and tell the group in what way they could be a resource. "I am Bud Jones, I
  ✓ speak Spanish
  ✓ am a computer buff
  ✓ am an attorney
  ✓ like to build things."

4

Group
Process

"Two's Company . . ."

Group Process is the interaction the group experiences. It is important because it reflects the continuity, maturity, productivity and honesty of the group.

People assume different kinds of roles within different groups, depending upon how safe they feel and how interested they are in the task. These roles generally fall into two categories: task or maintenance. When we assume *task roles,* they help the group to accomplish its objectives. They might do such things as coordinate, evaluate, give information and record information. *Maintenance roles* are the ones that help the group interact comfortably, so the task can be accomplished in the most productive manner. When people assume a maintenance role, they do things like encourage, mediate, agree with and congratulate individuals for good ideas. Some roles interfere with the task and maintenance of the group, such as: blocking others' comments, seeking recognition, dominating and avoiding the point.

By learning to be aware of group process—and helping others to be aware of it—people can accomplish more and feel better about the interaction. Several elements affect communication, and thus the effectiveness of the group process. These include:

Key Elements　1. Sense of significance (how much people feel a part of the group)

2. Sense of control (how people fit in and how competent they feel)

3. Sense of openness (how well liked they feel)

Content and Process   It is important to distinguish between *content* and *process*. *Content* is the "What" (agenda planning, the list of things the group needs to accomplish, etc.). *Process* is the "How," (brainstorming, lecture, slides, etc.). It is important to consider the process in terms of *directionality, participation, leadership* and *climate*.

✤ **Directionality**—Who is talking to whom (i.e., one to one, leader to group, or aimlessly).

✤ **Participation**—everyone should be actively involved.

✤ **Leadership**—It should facilitate interaction by encouraging and stimulating, rather than controlling the involvement.

✤ **Climate**—Should be one of cooperation rather than competition.

REASONS PEOPLE BELONG TO A GROUP

People do not associate with groups by chance, nor for purely altruistic reasons. People have needs. Membership in groups can satisfy any number of these needs.

1. A sense of being a part of something

2. A feeling of being wanted

3. An opportunity to work with others

4. A chance to give of one's self

5. A chance to use skills and talent

CHARACTERISTICS OF EFFECTIVE GROUPS

Each of the points listed below represents a goal worth considering. None is easy, nor comes without conscious effort. However, each is important to the effectiveness of group efforts.

✤ The leadership is appropriate to the needs of the group, and members have confidence in their leader.

✤ Growth and welfare of all members are considered.

✤ Goals are clear and shared by all.

✤ Group goals are compatible with individual goals.

✤ A defined timetable is used.

✤ Communication is open, frank and non-threatening.

✤ There is a sense of agreed priorities.

✤ The resources of each member are used satisfactorily.

✤ Goals are high but achievable.

✤ Members are capable of handling the tasks.

+ Decision-making procedures and authority are appropriate.

+ Conflict is dealt with openly.

+ Processes are routinely evaluated and results of those evaluations used.

ROLES TAKEN DURING GROUP DISCUSSION

Whether intentional or not, individuals involved in groups take on roles that affect their behavior and thus the group process. Some are task roles, some maintenance, and others self-serving. Many of the latter can have a negative effect on a group. It important to learn to recognize and deal with the various roles that exist in a group.

Task Roles

These help members get the job done:

+ **Information or opinion seeker:** Looks for facts and feelings on which to make decisions.

+ **Information or opinion giver:** Offers facts or generalizations that are authoritative, or relate to his own experience, pertinent to the group problem.

+ **Clarifier:** Rephrases for clarity and understanding.

+ **Initiator:** Proposes subjects, processes and direction.

+ **Elaborator:** Develops concepts more fully.

+ **Orienter:** Familiarizes group with new ideas, or new members with the group.

+ **Summarizer:** Summarizes what has occurred, points out departures from agreed-upon goals. Brings the group back to the central issues.

+ **Evaluator:** Subjects the accomplishments of the group to standards, or a set of standards. Questions the practicality, the logic and the facts.

Maintenance Roles

These help members feel satisfied and comfortable:

+ **Harmonizer:** Mediates differences among members. Attempts to reconcile disagreement and relieve tensions in conflict situations.

+ **Compromiser or mediator:** Proposes possible solutions or approaches that will meet most needs.

+ **Encourager:** Encourages others to continue to be involved.

+ **Supporter:** Has praise for everything and everyone.

❖ **Gate-keeper:** Keeps communication channels open by encouraging or facilitating the participation of quiet members or by proposing regulation of the flow of communication

Self-serving roles

❖ **Blocker:** May be negative and stubborn, resisting, disagreeing and opposing without reason.

❖ **Dominator:** Tries to assert himself by attempting to manipulate members of the group.

❖ **Resister:** Refuses to be put into a position of having to commit to anything.

❖ **Aggressor or criticizer:** Critical of everything and everyone (often to gain status).

❖ **Follower:** Goes along with anything.

❖ **Recognition seeker:** Works in various ways to call attention to himself through boasting, unusual acts or reporting of personal accomplishments.

NON-PRODUCTIVE BEHAVIOR

Some participants in groups regularly interfere with progress. The more common types of nonproductive behavior include:

❖ **Aggression:** working for status by criticizing or blaming others; showing hostility against the group or an individual; deflating the ego or status of others

❖ **Blocking:** interfering with the progress of the group by intentionally deviating from the subject of discussion; citing personal experiences unrelated to the problem; rejecting ideas without consideration; arguing excessively

❖ **Self-confessing:** using the group as a sounding board; expressing inappropriate personal feelings or points of view

❖ **Competing:** vying with others to produce the best ideas, to talk the most, to play the most roles, to gain the leader's favor

❖ **Recognition seeking:** attempting to call attention to one's self by loud or excessive talking, extreme ideas or unusual behavior

❖ **Special pleading**: introducing, or supporting suggestions related to personal concerns or philosophies; lobbying

❖ **Clowning:** joking; mimicking, disrupting the work of the group

❖ **Seeking sympathy:** trying to gain group members' sympathy for one's problems or misfortunes; deploring one's own ideas to gain support

❖ **Withdrawing:** acting indifferently or passively; resorting to excessive formality; daydreaming; doodling; whispering to others; wandering from the subject

❖ **Degrading:** acting in a manner that criticizes others

USING QUESTIONS TO STIMULATE DISCUSSION

A clear understanding of behaviors that help or deter progress can help the leader and increase the effectiveness of groups, organizations and communities. Good facilitation, in an interactive setting, decreases disruptive activity and increases productive involvement. See segment on Interaction Meeting, page 20.

A considerable responsibility falls to the group leader to involve all participants in discussions that affect the group. The following is intended as a guide to stimulate productive discussion.

Well-phrased questions stimulate group participants to think and motivate them to discuss the issues at hand. Three basic factors affect stimulation and motivation:

1) Choosing the right question

The right type of question is dependent upon the results sought. Categories of questions include:

✓ Factual questions:
  Used to get information.
  Good for discussion starters.
  Example: "How many people will you need?"

✓ Leading questions:
  Used to suggest an answer and have the group analyze.
  Helps to broaden the discussion.
  Example: "How would you feel about . . ."

✓ Clarifying questions:
  Used to challenge old ideas and develop new ones.
  To avoid snap judgments—To help find real causes or answers.
  Example: "What you are saying, then, is that committee apathy seems to be a problem."

✓ Hypothetical questions:
  Used to suggest or introduce leader's ideas into the discussion.
  To test conclusions.
  Example: "What would you think of . . . ?"

✓ Alternate questions:
  To decide between two or more points.
  To comparatively evaluate suggested solutions.
  Example: "Are breakfast or noontime meetings better?"

✓ Overhead (General):
  Directed at the entire group.
  Used to promote group thinking.
  Example: "What could we do about this?"

✓ Re-directed questions:
   Directed at leader but returned to the group
   Used to promote group activity
   Example: "That's a good question, John. How would you answer that in terms of your experience, Lynn?"

2) Framework of the question

✓ Be brief

✓ Cover a single point

✓ Relate the question

✓ Develop thinking from a constructive, positive point of view

✓ Use words that are natural to you

✓ Use words that have a clear meaning to the group

3) Directing the questions

✓ Direct questions to the group as a whole

✓ If no response, then select individuals to respond

✓ Allow sufficient time to reply

✓ Do not hesitate to restate the question if the group members appear confused

✓ Encourage members of the group to question one another

✓ Direct a hypothetical answer back to the group if you get no response

✓ Allow those who truly do not want to participate, to listen

Characteristics of a good question

Several characteristics of an effective question include:

✓ Have a specific purpose

✓ Have relationship to what is already known

✓ Be understood by the group

✓ Emphasize one point

✓ Require a definite answer

✓ Discourage guessing

✓ Encourage creative thinking

✓ Use why, where, when, who or how . . .

IMPROVING QUALITY OF PARTICIPATION

The productivity and congeniality of a group depends on the quality of the interaction, the participation. Groups are strengthened and enabled to work more efficiently if the members are:

✤ Conscious of the role/function needed at any given time

✤ Sensitive to and aware of the degree to which they can help meet their needs through what they do

✤ Willing to improve their range of role functions and skills in performing them

✤ Responsive to changing goals

✤ Aware that what *appears* to be non-functional behavior may not be

✤ Conscious of the positive possibilities of conflict aired within a group

✤ Concerned with the issues but also with the people who make things happen

HOW TO BE A BETTER GROUP DISCUSSION PARTICIPANT*

Some of the responsibility for effective group process must fall to the participants themselves. The material that follows includes ideas that can help individuals to become better group participants.

1. Come prepared. If material has been sent out in advance of the meeting, that's when it is supposed to be read. Time is often wasted at meetings filling in members who *should* already be informed.

2. Arrive on time and stay until the end of the meetings. To arrive late and leave early says, "I have better or more important things to do, this meeting is not a priority."

3. Be attentive. If you thought the meeting was important enough to attend, then attend to it when you are there. Be aware not only of *what* is being done, but *how* it is being done.

4. Be perceptive. In particular, become aware of the nonverbal messages that affect the group—room arrangement, seating arrangement, gestures, eye contact, body movements.

5. Help facilitate the discussion by taking an appropriate role in it. Avoid taking a self-serving role. If you see that a needed or helpful role is not being taken, take it yourself.

*Based on material by Marty Squire, consultant (used with permission)

6. Be a contributor. That is why you were asked to be a part of the group. If the group is a small one (up to 15 members), you have an even greater responsibility to contribute. See that your contribution is:

   ✓ Relevant to the discussion. If you have been actively listening, you lessen your chances of making irrelevant contributions. Use the "hook-on" technique of prefacing your comment with a reference to something said earlier by someone else.

   ✓ Offered at an appropriate time. Don't wait until the middle of a vote to come up with another alternative.

   ✓ Long enough to make your point. It has been found that contributions are more often too short rather than too long.

   ✓ Short enough to sustain the group's interest and attention. This means organizing your thoughts before you open your mouth. Don't belabor a point. Group members will remember this and then tune you out before you ever get started next time.

   ✓ Clear and easily understood. This may require rewording, defining terms, giving examples. Ask for feedback to let you know how you're doing.

   ✓ Open to evaluation and criticism. Once your comments are offered, they belong to the group, not to you. Let the members know they are free to do what they wish with the contribution. Sometimes it helps if you are one of the first to criticize or evaluate it.

   ✓ Informative and provocative. Don't bother if it isn't going to add something to the discussion or elicit further comments or ideas.

7. Don't be afraid to disagree. A certain amount of conflict is both inevitable and indispensable in a group discussion. The key is not to let it become personal. It is better to say "I believe that information may be incorrect." than "You are wrong." If you are going to criticize the idea or the outcome ("Things didn't turn out as well as they might have.", not "You sure let down your end."). If you are going to compliment, compliment the person, not the idea, the outcome, etc. ("You did a wonderful job on the golf tournament", not "The tournament was certainly a success this year."

8. Don't be afraid to be creative or innovative. Unfortunately, conformity is more often rewarded than creativity in an organization or group, but don't let this deter you. If you have gained the confidence and respect of the group, the members will usually be willing to hear a creative approach or innovative idea.

9. Give other creative ideas a fair shake. You may see these as wild but possibly that is the way someone saw your creative approach. Tolerance and open-mindedness are required, along with a willingness to try something new.

10. Become more tentative and less positive and/or dogmatic. Keep in mind that:
    ✓ Things are seldom either/or, always or never. There is usually some middle ground.
    ✓ Times, conditions, situations change. Don't treat any of them as though they never do.
    ✓ Your perception of reality, truth and goodness are usually at least a little different from everyone else's. This doesn't mean one is wrong and the other right. You will find interpersonal relationships in a group are much smoother when you preface more of your comments with, "To me," "As I see it," or "As far as I know."

Diversity   It is easy to see how some of us are different from others: we are taller or shorter, older, younger, of one race or another. But in group process these factors are of little significance.

For groups to work well together, consideration and concern must be shown for differences in temperament, values and priorities. These cannot be "seen." To help groups of people get along and work effectively together, the leader must create an environment where it is OK to be different where things aren't discussed in specific terms.

Most issues concerning groups can be viewed on a continuum. Some people may feel the consideration is of great importance, others will not hold it as a priority. Neither participant is 'right' or 'wrong'. The simply hold different points of view.

win/win   It is the challenge of the group leader to help each person feel their contribution counts. Group decisions are most effective when they represent a consensus. There will be a commitment to decisions if there is a sense of win/win.

5

Leadership

"Take Me to Your Leader"

*"Each time we ask more of ourselves than we think we can give . . .
and then give it . . . we grow."*
—Cicero

WHAT IS LEADERSHIP? In effective relationships, whether boss with employee, staff with volunteer, or chairman with committee, there must be a *balance*. This should reflect how much both are getting out of the relationship. If one or the other tends to gain more, and this is conspicuous to the other, productivity diminishes. The power one has over the other is rarely dependent on purse strings alone. It is also dependent on *each* person in the relationship receiving his or her needed degree of satisfaction and gratification. That is what volunteer work is all about.

A leader has only so much power over others. It is useful, positive, creative power if it includes finding the best people for the jobs, people who receive in return for their giving. Meeting the needs of others so they will meet yours, is one of the most important things a leader can do.

Leadership is situational. Different situations call for different styles of leadership. It is *the art of getting or inspiring people to do something* with the focus on *people.* By contrast, management deals with the allocation of resources associated with a *task.*

A leader is expected to act as a liaison between an individual and the organization. The behavior must be appropriate for the situation. And one style of leadership is not necessarily better than another. Can you imagine General Patton as leader of a sensitivity group—or Gandhi as a World War II commander? Groups differ and so must their leadership.

Leaders integrate the needs of followers with the goals of the organization by integrating people with tasks. They **transform potential into reality.** When selecting individuals to take on positions of leadership, people skills are more important than task skills or expertise in a specific area. Resource people should make up a committee, but not be expected to have leadership skills.

Leaders Focus on the Individual

Effective leaders model individual behaviors that nurture and encourage others. They:

✤ Look at the needs and strengths of individuals, "Build from Strength" (Drucker).

✤ Give people every opportunity to develop and utilize their talents and strengths.

✤ Provide a "climate" in which members are allowed to grow and accomplish the things of which they are capable.

✤ Provide every opportunity for members to identify their interests and abilities. When they know more about themselves they are better able to share this with the leader.

✤ Accept a refusal. Forcing members into tasks for which they have no enthusiasm will lead to frustration and disappointment for all.

✤ Avoid overstaffing—to the extent that the individuals begin to feel they really aren't needed.

✤ Specify clearly your expectation of members and listen to their expectations of you and others.

✤ "Never entrust opportunity to a non-resource." Leaders are aware of the capability and *dependability* of their members.

FIVE LEADERSHIP STYLES

People have a natural inclination to behave in a certain style. To be an effective leader it is important to consider the group to be led. When selecting a style, the maturity of the individuals and the group (in relation to the task) is the major concern.

Consideration should also be given to group members being led regarding their:

✤ Motivation/achievement/needs/expectations

✤ Willingness and ability to assume responsibility

✤ Education/experience/abilities

LEADERSHIP STYLES   Five leadership styles follow; the first two are leader-centered and the last two are group-centered. The less maturity a group demonstrates, the more direction it will need.

Authoritative   *Authoritative:* the leader decides and announces decisions.

Political   *Political:* the leader decides and *sells* the decision to the group.

Evaluative   *Evaluative:* the leader presents ideas and invites questions.

Participative   *Participative:* the leader presents alternatives and the group chooses from among them.

Laissez-faire   *Laissez-faire:* the group defines the boundaries and makes the decisions.

To be successful as a leader, all of the members of the group should be *involved in* and *buy into* the decisions that will affect them. "Bottoms up" is a good rule. Consult the people at the bottom before inflicting decisions on them. Effective leaders *listen* to the wishes of the group.

FUNCTIONS OF A LEADER   Each member has a responsibility to the rest of the group to help it to be effective. The leader coordinates the activities of the group. These include **task functions** (things that must be done if tasks are to be accomplished) and **maintenance functions** (things which help the group stay together and feel good about working together).

Task Functions

✤ **Initiating:** defining a problem, suggesting procedure for problem solving, making a proposal

✤ **Seeking Information or Opinions:** requesting background data, generating suggestions and ideas, gathering facts

✤ **Giving Information or Opinions:** offering facts or relevant information, stating beliefs, sharing new ideas or suggestions

✤ **Clarifying or Elaborating:** interpreting others' ideas; clearing up confusion, pointing out alternatives

✤ **Summarizing:** pulling related ideas together, establishing where the group is and what has been covered

✤ **Testing Agreement:** checking to see if the group has come to a consensus or has reached an understanding

These task functions will help in problem-solving and completing a task. But to be a productive, successful group, several maintenance functions also deserve consideration.

Maintenance Functions Include

✤ **Encouraging:** being responsive to and accepting of others; listening and trying to understand

✤ **Expressing Group Feelings:** being sensitive to how the group feels and being aware of inter-personal relationships within the group

✤ **Harmonizing:** attempting to reconcile opposing points of view. Tension must be reduced before group members can explore their differences objectively

✤ **Compromising:** admitting error if you make one, helping to maintain a group feeling, offering to compromise your own position to help the group

✤ **Gate-Keeping** (active participation): keeping the discussion a group discussion

✤ **Setting Standards:** code of operation adopted by the group—such as policy of letting everyone have a turn to be heard

In assuming an active role, every member has the responsibility to help create an effective group and to consider ideas, not their source. This is where Interaction Recording works so well. The chairman, as well as each individual, has a responsibility to listen for understanding, to contribute and make suggestions and to monitor himself so as not to dominate.

To put a group at ease, a leader can help members become better acquainted by using team-building exercises. It is also important that member see one another easily. Sit *with* the group yourself, if you are leader.

The leader should show enthusiasm and concern for the tasks facing the group. Help the members to realize that it is a job in which everyone's participation is needed. Promote team work by setting an example of friendliness, understanding, fairness and good will.

An effective leader encourages the group to consider all ideas fairly, so no one is afraid to make a suggestion. Give recognition to all and work to include everyone in your discussion.

SOME NEEDS OF PEOPLE IN GROUPS

If you want loyalty, honesty, interest and the best efforts from your group members, as a leader you must take into account that:

Sense of Belonging

They need a sense of belonging.

✓ A feeling that no one objects to their presence

✓ A feeling that they are sincerely welcome

✓ A feeling that they are honestly needed for themselves, not just for their hands, their money or to make the group larger.

Share in Planning

They need to have a share in planning the group goals. Their needs will be satisfied only when they feel that their ideas have had a fair hearing.

Realistic Goals They need to feel that the goals are within reach and that they make sense.

Provide Value They need to feel that what they are doing contributes something important to human welfare—that its value extends beyond the group itself.

Share in Rules They need to share in making the rules of the group—the rules by which they work toward their goals together.

Know Expectations They need to know in clear detail just what is expected of them so they can work confidently.

Challenge They need to have responsibilities that challenge, that are within range of their abilities and that contribute toward reaching their own goals.

Progress They need to see that progress is being made toward the goals the group has set and that they are making progress toward their own personal goals.

Information They need to be kept informed. What they are not up on, they may be down on. Lack of communication can lead to problems.

Confidence in Leader They need to have confidence in their leaders and officers— confidence based upon *assurance of consistent fair treatment, of recognition when it is due* and of *appreciation for steady, contributing membership.*

Rewards In brief, regardless of how much sense the situation makes to the leader, it must also make sense to the members. People continue to participate and contribute when they feel rewarded by the leadership.

These rewards include a chance to:

- feel useful—their only "pay" is satisfaction for a job well done. Praise from the leader is essential.

- use their special skills and talents.

- feel needed and wanted.

- confront local and national issues.

- experience personal growth and intellectual activity.

- be acknowledged as an important member of the team.

DELEGATING   It has been said that delegating is the hallmark of a successful leader. It is a method of getting work done with each member doing his part. Through delegating, a part of the responsibility is assigned to others who will help to find solutions. By doing this we also save time and develop leadership for the future.

❖ **Considerations before Delegating**
   ✓ Is the individual capable of handling the task?
   ✓ Will the individual take the responsibility seriously and feel a commitment to it?
   ✓ How critical is it to the total operation that this task be done well?

❖ **Criteria for Delegation**
   ✓ The ability of the individual to handle the task
   ✓ The importance of the task
   ✓ The consequence of failure
   ✓ The relationship of those involved

❖ **Advantages of Delegating**
   ✓ Develops a sense of belonging and importance in the members involved
   ✓ Encourages creativity, initiative and independence
   ✓ Inspires motivation (stimulates)
   ✓ Shares the power
   ✓ Offers an opportunity for growth and development and for others to observe this change
   ✓ Allows the leader freedom to oversee the total operation

❖ **Responsibilities of a leader**
   ✓ To assign tasks only to those qualified
   ✓ To make the assignment clear
   ✓ To assign authority to discharge the tasks
   ✓ To obtain the member's commitment to the task
   ✓ To provide needed resources to accomplish the task
   ✓ To offer encouragement and support

LEADERSHIP CONSIDERATIONS   It is essential for all members to have a clear understanding of how an auxiliary, agency or group is organized; how it operates and how it serves the community. It is especially important for those leaders in national, state and county positions.

The following questions may be helpful in making and implementing plans.

❖ What goals have you set for your group? Do you have a "mission statement?" A clear purpose?

❖ Are your current activities consistent with the purpose and goals?

✤ What is the degree of membership involvement in your current programs and projects?

✤ Are your activities in keeping with community needs? If not, what programs and projects might be substituted for your current activities?

✤ Does your present structure lend itself to effective programs and projects? If not, what changes should be made?

While you are fulfilling the duties as president or chairman, consider the future of your organization by building leadership qualities in others. Ongoing skill training is one of the best ways to develop the leadership potential of your members. Studies have shown that a chance to learn and to grow provides strong motivation for continued involvement by volunteers.

KEEPING DISCUSSIONS ON THE TOPIC

A leader must see to it that the key ideas are discussed and seek the maximum value out of each point made. The skill that helps most is *appropriate questioning*. Members of any group bring a variety of skills, information and degrees of motivation to the group. As a result, they do not always operate at peak efficiency without help from the leader.

When to ask questions

When to ask questions is particularly important. Here are five specific reasons:

1. **To focus the discussion:** Individual statements usually have a point. Statements themselves relate to a larger point being made. General discussion relates to an issue or to an agenda item. Use questions to determine a speaker's point or to determine the relationship of the point to the issue or agenda item.

2. **To probe for information:** Many statements need to be developed, supported or clarified. When the point appears important, the leader should pose questions to help bring the ideas into focus.

3. **To initiate discussions:** During a discussion, there are times when lines of development are apparently ignored, when the group seems ready to agree before sufficient testing has taken place. At such times, it is up to the leader to open up additional discussion and consideration by asking key questions.

4. **To deal with interpersonal problems:** Sometimes there is a need to air very personal feelings. When this happens, the leader should help an individual discuss her feelings, but not let her bias interrupt the real purpose of the discussion. Guard against letting the group attack a person instead of the information that is being presented. When this happens, the leader has the burden of focusing attention of the group on the idea, instead of the source.

5. **To choose / commit / decide:** Questions help members select from a number of options, to commit to responsibility or to decide on direction.

Questions by themselves will not make a discussion. In fact, some questions can hurt the discussion that is taking place. An effective leader uses questions sparingly, but decisively. She develops sensitivity to the needs of the group members. She can read tone and inflection and body language, as well as words.

RESPONSIBILITIES OF A LEADER

To perform effectively as a leader, remember that the position brings with it the following responsibilities:

- ✤ Listen!
- ✤ Contribute
- ✤ Do not dominate
- ✤ Show enthusiasm
- ✤ Put group at ease

- ✤ Discourage criticism
- ✤ Be fair
- ✤ Give recognition
- ✤ Promote team work
- ✤ Focus on problem or task

CONSIDERATIONS FOR LEADERS*

Philip Crosby offers a number of concise points with regard to Leadership. These are worth noting:

- ✤ There are no easy solutions.

- ✤ Prevention is a future thing.

- ✤ People are more important to situations than things.

- ✤ Embarrassed kittens become tigers.

- ✤ People rise to a challenge, if it is given.

- ✤ A person's loyalty is a function of how he feels he is appreciated.

- ✤ Success depends on controlling your environment.

- ✤ Dedication is wanting your thing to happen more than they want it to happen.

- ✤ A person's self-esteem is his most important possession. Don't destroy it.

- ✤ Most major jobs can be broken down into several manageable tasks.

- ✤ If something is inevitable, acknowledge it and use it to your best advantage.

*Based in part on material by Philip B. Crosby in *The Art of Getting Your Own Sweet Way,* McGraw Hill, © 1972, Philip B. Crosby (used with permission)

✦ Volunteers don't work for money—they work for good feelings.

✦ If you don't ask the right questions, you won't get the right answers.

✦ Volunteers are more committed to tasks they have helped develop

✦ Learn from your mistakes and keep useful records for your successor.

✦ Time invested in planning pays off in the end.

✦ What you feel is not always apparent to others.

✦ Communication and understanding take effort.

✦ Prevention is planned anticipation.

✦ If a worker does not understand *why* he is doing something, he probably won't do it very well.

✦ Always show more concern for the people than the task. They get the job done for you.

✦ Creative ideas flourish in a free and open environment.

✦ Build on the past; don't be tied to it.

✦ Change is the very thing we *can* count on; are you preparing to deal with it?

✦ The future will be very different from the past, like it or not.

✦ If you don't invest time in doing it *right* now, when will you have time to do it over?

✦ Are you helping those around you to grow and become future leaders?

✦ If you expect positive results, cultivate a positive attitude in yourself and co-workers.

LEADERSHIP DEVELOPMENT Unless you develop the leadership potential within those with whom you work, you are destined to work too hard yourself! Everything will need your attention. In your absence things will come to a virtual halt. And, until you develop a competent replacement, you may be cast in your current position indefinitely. It is an engraved invitation for burnout to set in. Here are several suggestions for developing a capable understudy.

✦ Keep your assistant thoroughly posted on your plans and the progress of these plans.

✦ Teach him the habit of giving you frequent progress reports.

✦ Provide opportunity for independent thinking. Ask that he bring you possible solutions to any problems he encounters.

✤ Place responsibility on the assistant gradually. Add one new assignment at a time.

✤ Build up his sense of responsibility. Delegate complete responsibility for specific tasks. If he makes a suggestion as good as yours, use it.

✤ Hold him accountable for his responsibilities. Make your expectations clear.

✤ Make him feel free to ask for new responsibilities. Show that you are anxious for him to develop new skills.

✤ Back him up. Give your support publicly. If it is necessary to criticize, do it privately.

✤ Teach him to admit mistakes promptly. Let him know you want to hear about mistakes before they lead to other problems.

✤ Help him learn to take criticism constructively. Let him know you speak of these issues only because you care about him and the quality of the job that is done.

CHARACTERISTICS OF SUCCESSFUL ORGANIZATIONS

Organizations that succeed year after year with outstanding performance are those that have a unifying philosophy of self-determination and high hope. They *believe* in their ability to determine their own destiny. They do not cower in the face of obstacles such as a poor economy, too few volunteers and unemployment.

In successful organizations there is a sense of purpose to all action and this creates a sense of identity among the staff and volunteers. Each feels he is a critical part of an integrated whole. The organizational purpose is an extension of individual purpose and this allows for the satisfaction of feelings of self-worth.

There is also a commitment to the *people*, not just the *task* at hand. There is concern for the well-being and growth of co-workers. Opportunity is provided for individuals to make a meaningful contribution. The tasks are as important for the development of the individual as for the organization's goal.

The prevailing *attitude* that permeates the group is positive and constructive. This has a tremendous affect on the ultimate success of the group. The climate is set by the leader. Succesful organizations invest time and energy in listening to and meeting the needs of the staff, Board and volunteers who deliver the program. It is the leader who facilitates this.

Key Elements

Organizations capable of inspired performance seem to have several key elements at work:

- ✤ A sense of purpose
- ✤ An alignment of individuals around this purpose
- ✤ A concern for personal performance and growth
- ✤ A commitment to creating a positive working environment
- ✤ An effective structure
- ✤ A clear line of authority and a strong, sensitive leader
- ✤ A level of communication that integrates reason and intuition, allows for creativity and clarifies expectations
- ✤ A sincere interest in maintaining good work relationships

Qualities of Leadership

Successful organizations are lead by individuals who:

- ✤ Are willing to make trade-offs
- ✤ Work from set goals
- ✤ Are effective communicators
- ✤ Are perceptive and sensitive to the group and their needs
- ✤ Are good at integrating various interests and priorities
- ✤ Are creative and adaptable
- ✤ Provide a positive role model
- ✤ Acknowledge the efforts of all
- ✤ Tactfully allow for differences
- ✤ Demonstrate patience and professionalism
- ✤ Can move beyond their own biases

Organizations ultimately succeed because those in charge have managed to bring out the best in all involved. Groups chaired by individuals concerned about the people are in a position to manage the tasks effectively. When the focus is exclusively on the tasks to be accomplished there is a great risk that it may never be accomplished. It is *people* who make things happen. A strong, successful leader approaches all tasks from the perspective of how the individual's needs can be met in the process.

6

Motivation

"What Makes You Tick?"

"If you want to gather honey, don't kick over the beehive."
—Dale Carnegie

Motivation is often used to mean *stimulation*. You *can't* motivate others. If you are very clever you *can* stimulate them to action, but their *motivation* must come from *within*. Any attempt to motivate others will be met with the same frustration experienced when you attempt to push a string.

In the volunteer world it is secondary re-enforcers—elements other than paychecks—that move people to action. Those in business realized some time ago if the paycheck is the only motivation an employee brings to his job, then quality will likely diminish! With volunteers the concern needs to be with feelings: recognition, approval, acceptance and love. These are important in any work situation, but *essential* for a volunteer's satisfaction with his job. Without these, people are rarely motivated to maintain a high standard of performance.

Committee members invest an element of feeling in their work and a good chairman responds to that investment with empathy and provides meaningful payoffs. This can be by way of individual recognition or public praise. It can be with a gratifying assignment.

A volunteer leader needs to recognize that a person's self-esteem is his most treasured possession. Handle it with care. A volunteer will move away from an assignment if he is belittled or made to feel inadequate. An employee may stay on under such a circumstance. But he would hardly be motivated to produce the best work.

LOGIC AND EMOTION

It is a key concept in motivation to remember that when you are dealing with people, you are not dealing with creatures of logic but creatures of *emotion*—creatures filled with prejudices and motivated by pride and vanity. Condemning and criticizing people will only put them on the defensive. When this happens, an individual will try every means to justify himself. His *pride* will be wounded, as will his sense of importance. This arouses resentment.

So, instead of dwelling on drawbacks and weaknesses of volunteers, try to understand them as people. Try to figure out *why* they do what they do.

According to Freud, how you get your feelings of importance tells a great deal about you, about your character. Some achieve their desire to be great by giving of time, talent or money; others, by ruling over others (either positively or negatively). The need to feel significant is an important consideration in stimulating others to *motivate* themselves.

The word motivation comes from the Latin *movere*—to move toward satisfying a need. It is a response to a stimulus. An example I like is to think in terms of a flower seed. We know it needs light, water and food to grow into a healthy flower. We can supply these things, but we can't motivate that seed to utilize them. Each seed is capable of becoming a different kind of flower. In the best of conditions it can bloom—but a daisy seed will only become a daisy, never a rose.

Motivation induces action, it provides the *motive*, or inner urge. There must be an inner urge to do things differently, or to do things at all, if there is to be motivation. If you are working with a group of seemingly uncommitted volunteers perhaps it is time to ask a few questions. Consider:

MOTIVATION CONSIDERATIONS

1. What specific goals for achievement do they have? What goals do you have?

2. Using positive imagery (imagining success), what does their success look like? What is your mental picture of success?

3. What is their perception of the situation? What is yours?

4. What do they see as their responsibility in this situation? And yours? How do *you* see their responsibility? And yours?

5. What action do they see to take that could bring about positive results? What do they see you doing? What actions do you see that they could be doing? And you?

6. Are they willing to make a commitment to change or action? Are you?

As a leader the challenge is to inspire interest in positive behavior and to light the way with practical, non-threatening examples of how things could be different and more productive. Be open to change and criticism yourself. The only person you can change is yourself. But by changing what you do you will change what you get in response.

ENVIRONMENT When you think of co-workers, think of providing an *environment* that will help others to meet their needs. This will help in their motivation. This is where an attempt to understand the individual is so important. For example, if one volunteer continually offers her services but never completes the task, this behavior will affect your entire group. When you ask yourself why she does this, you may begin to realize that she simply needs recognition. Your challenge is then to create an environment where she can receive recognition for positive behavior.

Removing causes for dissatisfaction that relate primarily to environmental conditions does not guarantee future satisfaction. Satisfaction is more than the absence of irritation. Satisfaction is tied to factors intrinsic to the job, the job *content*.

SATISFACTION (Job Content)	DISSATISFACTION (Job Environment)
✓ Sense of achievement	✓ Agency policies (if disagreeable)
✓ Recognition	✓ Relationship with supervisor (if negative)
✓ Job itself	✓ Working condition (if poor)
✓ Responsibility	✓ Relationship with co-workers (if tense)
✓ Advancement	✓ Little recognition for effort

ORIENTATION Early orientation for new members can greatly influence later enthusiasm within your group. Preplanning a clear-cut set of objectives for what you hope to accomplish and within what time period can assure you a larger percentage of happy volunteers in years to come.

First, be sure to describe what is expected of the individual and show how he can develop and grow as a result of his experiences with your organization.

Second, help him to understand the mission and policies of the organization and its primary reason for being, as well as how he can be a worthwhile addition to the group.

Third, and perhaps most importantly, seek to make your new member feel welcome and a part of the group as a whole. If he is anxious to become active immediately, help to find an opportunity suited to his talents.

MOTIVATION AND MANAGEMENT

Richard Anderson, in *Motivation—the Master Key*, refers to a manager's "motivation quotient"—resulting from two factors: first, your attitude, and second, your management methods.

Community leaders need to begin to see themselves as managers of sorts and to set out to acquire many of the useful tools applied in business. One such point is "give co-workers more personal attention than job attention once they know what they're doing." This includes building a sense of team. Become sensitive to the needs of your fellow co-workers and volunteers.

There are three basic methods for stimulating people to action. First, you can drive them by unrelenting pressure. Second, you can inspire them to give their all for you as their leader. (This works effectively only for the charismatic leader). Third, you can stimulate them to develop their own capabilities and perform to their own satisfaction. A good manager can inspire motivation. He or she cannot *impose* it.

Reasons may be compelling, but the way people *feel* affects their conduct more than the way they *think*.

Constructive Criticism

Constructive criticism must be considered routine. As suggested in Chapter 11, *Quality Management*, each task should be evaluated upon conclusion, if not periodically during the process. Members should expect help along the way, not a "put down" at the end. Remember, your criticism always should be of the action, not the individual. "What" concerning the plan or approach didn't work? Don't be personal. This system is designed to alleviate personality conflicts. Always deliver criticism in private and praise in public.

Recognize Performance

It is equally important to *recognize* outstanding performance. Reward real workers publicly and when possible tangibly, even if it is just with a certificate. Make it a practice to recognize achievement. It is very encouraging.

If you expect people to act on what you say, your own conduct must show that you believe it. You must also communicate that you believe in them and give them adequate tools and explanations to handle the assignment.

Keep in mind that your actions speak louder than words. If you truly want to convey one message, then your own behavior must not be in conflict with your words. You can't ask for dependability and follow-through from your committee members if you perpetually fail to come through or produce as promised.

CLARIFYING EXPECTATIONS

Parent study classes teach that a child will become what you accuse him of being. Tell a child he is lazy and he will prove you right. Tell him he is thoughtful and he will prove this to be true. So it is with committee people. They behave pretty much as you expect them to.

If you let people know you are counting on them and if you demonstrate this confidence by giving them opportunity, the few disappointments you have will be abundantly balanced by the many bonuses of surprising achievement. If you want to draw out the best in people, you must look for it. Additionally, seek to empower others and help them to succeed. Avoid standing idly by watching trouble brew.

Knowing why the behavior exists gives you clues as to how to deal with a problem. Your next step might be simply to try to come up with ways to meet this person's need for recognition. In doing so, you serve the group as well.

MOTIVATION QUESTIONS

Periodically it might be useful to present an opportunity for your members to express *why* they belong to your group. Do you know? It may seem obvious, but then again, it may produce surprises. You could give each of your members 5 index cards at a meeting and have each fill out one, in answer to each of the following questions:

✓ Why did you join this group?
✓ Are you finding what you hoped to find?
✓ How satisfying do you find this experience?
✓ Why do you continue to belong?
✓ How could the group be better for you?

Then, recording on a large flip chart, page 22, have members share their responses—tallying the most frequently mentioned answers. From here you can begin to compare actual experience to members' expectations and then work on ideas for things you might do to make the group more satisfying to most members.

This is an effective tool only when applied to small groups (fewer than 30) or when done in committee. It is important that everyone be able to see the chart.

FEELINGS PEOPLE HAVE ABOUT GROUPS

The following is a list of fairly universally accepted feelings people have about groups. People want:

✓ To be free
✓ To work through a democracy
✓ To find diversity more than conformity
✓ To be effective
✓ To grow in a feeling of value

Bottoms Up is the Bottom Line

When you let others express their hopes and expectations, you increase communication, understanding and the likelihood of a commitment to the very things you need. Consult your volunteers and show respect for their advice. To get things done, set up a challenge and provide a chance for self-expression and success. "Bottoms up is the bottom line." Let changes begin with those who will be most affected by the decisions.

Ensure success   Instead of handing out edicts and orders, present your wishes as questions and let the members answer them. This shares the responsibility for decision-making, establishes the challenge and provides an opportunity to assure understanding. Most people can't be *sold*, you have to let them *buy*.

"Bait the hook to suit the fish."   The only way we can get volunteers to do anything is by giving them what they want. Therefore, understanding your co-workers is of great importance. Carnegie uses an example of being very fond of strawberries and cream, also of fishing. When he fishes, he doesn't use strawberries as a lure—just because he likes strawberries. He motivates the fish with what *they* want—worms! To quote Lloyd George, "Bait the hook to suit the fish."

—Lloyd George

Remember, you can make more friends in two weeks by being interested in others than you can in two years trying to get others interested in you. Always make the other person feel important. In any confrontation, always let the other "save face." If you have your way but lose all of your people or their backing—what will you really have to show for your effort?

Also, it is always easier to listen to unpleasant things after we've heard some praise of our good points. If you must find fault, spend a little time on some *good* aspect of the issue before you get to the *bad*.

We all know we are producing only a small portion of what we are capable, even in the best of circumstances. When we find ourselves in situations of conflict and frustration, we produce even less. And, on the more positive side, with inspiration and challenge we can produce beyond anyone's expectations.

Commitment   Any activity that *stimulates* (the key word!) a volunteer's natural drive will always inspire greater imagination, resourcefulness and commitment. It is up to the chairmen, the leaders, to cultivate the best in their committee members by controlling the atmosphere of the meetings and applying the talents of the members. Ultimately *how* you do what you do is just as important as *what* you do. Control things not people.

CONSIDERATIONS FOR ADMINISTRATORS   The Center for Creative Management cites five important points for their administrators:

   ✓ Create an environment where each person finds the work for which she is best suited and wants most to do.

   ✓ Give people the tools they need to do their jobs.

   ✓ Challenge them to do their best while giving them the opportunity to do it.

   ✓ Reward them equitably for their efforts.

   ✓ Offer them an opportunity to learn, to grow and to advance.

People are not always in a position to select the individuals they would most like for their committees, but when you are being asked to serve, give serious thought to the requirements of the position. Will the job suit *your* talents? You will be motivated to achieve your best if the job suits *your* interests and skills.

This handbook is about how you can help yourself and other people achieve the most out of your/their volunteer involvement. As a chairman you need to remember you can't stimulate others to do their best for you if they don't bring enthusiasm to the challenge. If you are a committee person, you will only be motivated to produce if you sincerely want to become involved—not to please someone else, or because you should, or because no one else will if you don't. Your motivation must be to express yourself and use your talents—as Carl Rogers says—to "self-actualize."

As a chairman, you wouldn't want to assign Introverted Ivan to the task of selling ads for your program, and relegate Gregarious Glenda to address envelopes. As a committee person, when asked to work on a project, consider all the options and offer your assistance in the area most suited to your needs, your talents and your schedule. That is not selfish—that makes sense! It guarantees your interest and commitment. There will always be jobs that seem just awful to some that others would enjoy.

MATCHING SKILLS WITH JOBS

Matching people's skills to their jobs is vital. Many organizations have nominating committees. These can be treacherous assignments. It is possible they will be expected to talk others into doing things. But this need not be the case.

A really good nominating committee has access to information about each of the members of the organization, preferably provided by the members themselves through a questionnaire. If people are given the opportunity to indicate relevant experience, as well as areas of interest, the matching of people to jobs of their preference will practically guarantee motivation and greatly increase the chances of success for a project.

It is important to *define* the jobs. This is so the volunteer understands what is expected of him, how long he has to do the job, and how much help he will get. It is also helpful to note what skills are required—and what skills are apt to be acquired. (see page 41)

The selection of a group's Board is probably of greatest importance. With a wise choice of key people, great things are possible. If your Board is made up of committee chairmen, each should be allowed, (where possible) to seek a committee of people who will complement his or her personality, skill, interest and temperament.

Agency Boards are generally made up of representatives from the community at large. Where possible the nominating committee should work closely with the current Board to generate ideas of individuals to approach—for concrete reasons. Consideration should be given to *who* approaches the prospective board member to make the appeal. While it is important to avoid conning people into positions, there may be individuals who are more apt to show a sincere interest if someone they care about and admire makes the contact.

Common Values

Remember that if the whole committee is of like interests, talents and attitudes, little of great value is apt to be accomplished. On the other hand, if the group is too varied, it could become so divisive as to destroy itself. When there are common values, the group will work well on mutually agreed-upon goals, with members stimulating and challenging one another—because there is no tension or pressure to compete. They will want to complement the other instead. There will be *cooperation* because the group realizes that they will gain from the success of one another.

The Peter Principle
"In a hierarchy, every employee tends to rise to his level of incompetence."
—Dr. Lawrence J. Peter

Business people are beginning to learn that craftsmen need not be promoted to supervisor when what they do best requires different skills. Volunteers, too, can come to understand the requirements of various positions so as not to take assignments for the glory of the title, but to stick to the things they do best (or take advantage of training to gain new skills).

This is not to say people should not move beyond their "comfort zone"— rather, not to do so until the needed skills have been mastered. Conferences and workshops are offered frequently in most large cities where it is possible to gain new skills that will help qualify volunteers for new challenges. Isn't that what we really want? Don't give people jobs because they need them or for the experience. But give them opportunities to become skilled in varied areas so they become *qualified* to be considered for new positions.

If you know what positions you would like to hold, determine what skills are needed to do the job well and set about achieving these. Then let others know that you would like to be considered for the position and that you have gone out of your way to prepare for the challenge.

A really successful organization selects leaders on the basis of their capabilities, rather than seniority. Organizations need to move away from the idea that the most-senior members *ought* to be president. When people begin to be recognized for their performance and capabilities, others become motivated to expand their skills. Incentive is destroyed if a few are always given the key positions.

When considering new members and how people are motivated to join in the cause that we think is so worthwhile, remember to look first at *their* needs. Too often people are recruited simply because they have the time or a secondary interest. This tends to produce an organization top-heavy with numbers, a small percentage of whom really care about giving their all.

Opportunities to Contribute   Beyond the problems of great numbers joining with little real interest— you also risk having more people than you actually need. Even if they were highly motivated when they signed up, that motivation will diminish rapidly if they aren't given frequent opportunities to make important contributions to the cause. There always will be those who want to say they belong and to appear on the roster or letterhead. They really want to do *nothing*. Organizations need to recognize and reward those who joined for other reasons and who work to maintain a high degree of satisfaction with their association.

Introspection   People sometimes resign from groups, not because they no longer believe the cause was good, but because *they* have changed. Their needs changed, and their goals changed. And, as they look at the prospect of meeting and fulfilling these needs, they realize that it will not be through these groups. So it is time to move on. This requires considerable introspection and coming to grips with *who one is* and *what one needs* to be happy and fulfilled.

It is important to be aware of the needs of our volunteers, to listen to their viewpoints, to create an environment that will inspire and challenge. Provide training opportunities that assure growth and you build future leadership.

NEEDS OF VOLUNTEERS*   If my best efforts are desired, my leader will know that, as a volunteer, I need . . .

✦ To be given *Confidence:*
  ✓ To feel that I'm trusted in work assigned to me.
  ✓ To be told results desired but not "How to do it."

✦ To be given *Recognition* when earned:
  ✓ To be acknowledged for my efforts, ideas and work.
  ✓ To be known, understood and to have concern shown for me as an individual.

✦ To have *Delegation* follow accepted guidelines:
  ✓ To have reasons for a task explained clearly.
  ✓ To have accountabilities clearly prescribed.

✦ To get *Feedback*—and be asked for my thoughts and ideas:
  ✓ To have one-to-one sessions on "how I am doing" (my progress).
  ✓ To be informed on the progress of my organization.
  ✓ To find progress toward *my* personal goals.

*By Dr. J. Donald Phillips, Chancellor Emeritus, Hillsdale College, Hillsdale, Michigan (used with permission)

❖ To be *Involved,*
  ✓ To be allowed to share in decisions that affect me—as often and as much as possible.
  ✓ To be kept "in" on all appropriate information.
  ✓ To have opportunities for fair hearings.
  ✓ To feel free to ask questions without intimidation.

❖ To gain a personal *Sense of Belonging:* (see all other items)

❖ To be *Challenged*—to be given the opportunity:
  ✓ To create, discover, compete.
  ✓ To have changes in tasks for new challenges and satisfactions.

❖ To find *Relevance*—to know:
  ✓ "Why?" "Why me?" "Why at this time?" "Why important?"
  ✓ Whether I may be contributing to something larger than self, and that goals make sense to me.

❖ To gain *Increasing Understanding:*
  ✓ Of self, of supervisors, of organization (philosophy, policies, procedures).
  ✓ By having opportunities to work with challenges, people, things.

❖ To develop *Confidence* in my superior, I'd like to see:
  ✓ Constancy in method of operation.
  ✓ Enthusiasm, a good example, fairness, ability, and above all, integrity.
  ✓ "Your greatest opportunity is to match people with the routines they enjoy.'

CONSENSUS Group consensus inspires motivation because the members feel their input has been acknowledged. They have had a say in how things will be. On appropriate levels it is wise to seek the feelings and opinions of those who will be affected by decisions. This does not mean to open any whole topic for debate, but on a committee level to come to an agreement on several possible options. Work from the general, to a specific committee-recommended proposal.

The Environment Some situations simply will not stimulate volunteers to creative participation. Many committee meetings, by necessity, are held in homes. When this is necessary, try to clear the surroundings of distractions. Arrange for a neighbor to watch your preschooler and discourage others from bringing their children. Every distraction is a drawback to a successful meeting.

In Girl Scout Leader Training "cooperative sitters" are frequently engaged. Those are often junior or senior scouts. This is a great idea. A sitter is hired to be on the premises, usually a church, *in another room.*

Each leader pays her in accordance with the number of children she brings. The little ones have a wonderful time and they know mom is nearby. There are other children to play with and it alleviates the problem of *finding* a sitter. It is a windfall to the sitter who would ordinarily have just one paying customer.

Speaking of Girl Scouts, the girls themselves can often be hired to sit for such things as P.T.A. meetings. Their services can be used as a fundraiser for their troop, or without pay as a community service. Not having children in attendance can add greatly to the motivation of the group.

A leader's stock in trade is *people.* The material resources are made vital by the actions of people, and the leader is the inspiration to these people. This is true in the workplace and the volunteer world. Every chairman is dependent upon his committee to allocate time and resources in a manner productive to the cause. The leader's challenge is to create an environment in which they will thrive.

Identity   Finally, volunteers need *identity.* And they will do something to achieve this feeling. It is up to the chairman to help each achieve it in a positive, productive manner. Remember that all behavior is rooted in the need structure of the individual.

Satisfaction of one's need for self-esteem leads to a feeling of self-confidence, worth, strength, capability and adequacy. To cultivate this in others, recognize every opportunity to build up this feeling. By doing this, co-workers tackle their assignments with a greater feeling of usefulness. The end result is that they are challenged to capacity and their efforts reflect well on the leadership.

HIGH ACHIEVEMENT NEEDS*   People with high achievement needs tend to want:

❖ Immediate, concrete feedback; to know as soon as possible how well they are doing so they can adjust their performance to meet their personal needs and goals and those of the organization.

❖ Moderate risk-taking situations where there is a personal challenge, but not one left to fate. They like situations where they can be assured of success as long as they are doing their best.

❖ Personal responsibility for their own success or failure. When they fail at a task they want to know why, not be given an excuse. They learn from evaluating past performance so as not to repeat their mistakes.

❖ Work that is challenging and structured so as to provide feedback on an ongoing basis.

❖ An opportunity to develop positive relationships with others while dealing with challenging work.

❖ Latitude to make decisions about the process of the work.

*Based on material by Kolb, Rubin & McIntyre in *Organizational Psychology, an Experimental Approach,* 1979 .

To inspire motivation within others, be supportive, clarify your expectations, give constructive, ongoing feedback and ask opinions. Involve people from the bottom up. Allow those affected by a decisions need to be a part of the decision-making process. Offer opportunity for growth and be prepared to enlarge both the scope of individual jobs and the responsibility as well.

People want to be appreciated and to know that what they do is significant. Most would like increased challenges and responsibilities. They need the encouragement and assurance of someone they admire and they need high expectations. Expect the best and you are more apt to get the best. Set the stage for enthusiasm and success and you will nurture it in others. Provide a fertile environment in which those around you may grow. Be a mentor. Share your skills and talents. Be an inspiration to others!

MOTIVATION FACTORS

Motivating others involves an awareness of their values, needs, interests and self concept. Each of these have a great affect on the motivation of an individual.

Values

Values influence personal decisions because they are tied to the individual's priority system. Those who value their time will fall by the wayside if they find meetings are a waste of their time. Members who value *social interaction* may drop out if they find meetings are *too* structured and business-like.

Needs

Needs are those inner urges that cause people to act. When things are *comfortable there is no need to look for change or alternatives*. However, if things are stressful, members move to change things. They may move 'out' to get away, or 'up' because a creative, challenging stress is at work.

Interests

Interests differ from one member to another, and from one group to another. Though one common cause may bring people together, individual skills and talents account for the activity within this frame that will be of interest to each member.

Self-Concept

Self-Concept is significant in that the appeal of the group or specific task hinges, to a great extent, on how the individual feels he fits into this picture, whether he is 'up' to it or even 'above' it. To motivate (stimulate) an individual the activity must be congruent with the person's self-concept.

DEFENSE MECHANISMS

Many times people hide their feelings by using defenses. Each defense serves to avoid naming the feeling that is being experienced. We sometimes employ defensive mechanisms to hide "the truth" from ourselves. To expose the real feelings takes honest inquiry into why the individual is demonstrating the particular response. It always relates to the pursuit of a need—and often is founded in the attempt to maintain self-image. It may be very disconcerting for people to discover they are not who they would like to think they are. It can make people uncomfortable to confront the causes of their behavior. But it is the only way to intercept non-constructive behavior such as defense mechanisms represent.

SOME DEFENSES THAT PEOPLE USE:

Rationalizing	Agreeing
Justifying	Displaying anger
Projecting	Minimizing
Blaming, accusing	Evading, dodging
Judging, moralizing	Defying
Intellectualizing	Attacking
Analyzing	Withdrawing
Exclaiming	Verbalizing, talking
Theorizing	Threatening
Generalizing	Frowning
Quibbling	Glaring
Switching subjects	Staring
Complying	Joking, laughing

VOLUNTEER INTEREST

The following points are made to help you to recognize why volunteers lose interest. The second list is factors that encourage people to remain committed.

Why Volunteers Lose Interest

✤ Discrepancies between their expectations of membership or the task, and the reality of the situation

✤ No feeling of making a difference—no praise or reward

✤ Assignments too routine with no variety

✤ Lack of support from co-workers

✤ Little prestige related to the task or group

✤ No chance for personal growth

✤ No chance to meet personal needs

✤ Too little chance to demonstrate initiative or creativity

✤ Tension among co-workers

Why Volunteers Remain Committed

Reasons *why* people remain committed include:

✤ They feel appreciated

✤ They can see their presence does make a difference

✤ There is a chance for advancement

✤ There is opportunity for personal growth

✤ They receive private and public recognition

✤ They feel capable of handling the tasks offered

✤ There is a sense of belonging and teamwork among co-workers

✤ They are involved in the administrative process: problem-solving, decision-making and objective-setting

✤ They recognize that something significant is happening because the group exists

✤ Their personal needs are being met

BASIC PSYCHOLOGICAL NEEDS

The following needs are basic to the psychological development and growth of people. Volunteer leaders will do well to periodically assess how well they are doing in creating an environment that will satisfy these basic needs:

Acceptance
To feel that the attitude of others toward them is positive

Achievement
To acquire, gain, receive, win or strive to accomplish

Affection
To be loved, cherished, emotionally wanted for their own sake

Approval
To have others' behavior toward them demonstrate that they are viewed satisfactorily

Belonging
To feel a part of a group or organization

Conformity
To be like others, to avoid marked departure from the mode

Dependence
For emotional support from others

Independence
To do things free from external control by friends, family, associates or others

Mastery-dominance
To control, to be in power, to lead, to manage

Recognition
To be noticed, to become known

Self-realization
To function at one's ability level

To be understood
To feel rapport with co-workers and others

If, as an organizational leader, you observe disruptive or negative behavior, it is probably because one of the basic psychological needs is not being met. If you are concerned with motivating (stimulating) your members it will require that you invest time and energy in creating an environment where individuals can meet these needs. If your efforts are focused exclusively on the tasks at hand, the negative factors may be worsened by lack of attention.

MASLOW'S HIERARCHY OF NEEDS* Maslow's Hierarchy (below) has long been used to show how needs work. An individual is not motivated to satisfy needs on any level without having the needs on all levels below satisfied first. Once the lower level needs are satisfied, they no longer serve as motivators.

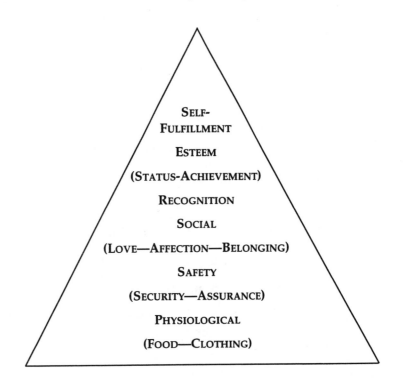

*Adapted from *Motivation & Personality* A. H. Maslow, Harper, New York, 1964, (used with permission).

FACTORS THAT MOTIVATE ME

This checklist is intended as an assessment tool for individual volunteers. Indicate 5 items from the list below that you feel are the most important in motivating you.

❑ I enjoy it; it is interesting.

❑ Others are doing it.

❑ It leads to recognition from others.

❑ I have the skill to do it .

❑ I feel the task is important.

❑ It is easy

❑ I feel trusted and respected in it.

❑ I have the opportunity to do a good job.

❑ I am expected to do it.

❑ I have a chance to help with the planning.

❑ I get along well with others involved in the task.

❑ I have a good supervisor or leader.

❑ I have sufficient amount freedom in doing it.

❑ I have the opportunity to take responsibility.

❑ I have the opportunity to grow and develop on the job.

❑ I have the opportunity to meet others.

❑ I have the opportunity to make career contacts.

❑ I can do most of the work at home.

❑ There is a routine I can count on.

❑ (Other)

Now, when offered a volunteer challenge, consider if the position offers the opportunity for satisfaction, in keeping with what you have listed as important.

This tool can be used in a training session focused on motivation and how to assure involvement and satisfaction of objectives. A review of responses will show that everyone has a different set of factors that are viewed as important. No one factor is more important as a consideration for groups. They are simply different for different people.

© 1994 Emily Kittle Morrison, *Leadership Skills*, Fisher Books, Tucson, Arizona

7

Communication

"Am I Getting Through?"

To Communicate: "To impart to another, to make known"
—Webster's

I know that you believe you understand what you think I said but . . .
I am not sure you realize that what you heard is not what I meant.

To truly communicate, understanding must take place. By definition communication involves at least two people: the sender and the receiver. As a sender your message is filtered through assumptions about what you want to share and attitudes about the message itself. As a receiver what is heard is filtered through your own set of priorities. You are, at least to some degree, selective in your attention.

Truth To a greater or lesser extent (as determined by the situation and relationship) people are willing and able to communicate only what they perceive. *Truth* is based on what we are aware of, but our *behavior* is affected by *unconscious beliefs* as well. These include all the things people choose to *not* know about because generally, self-discovery can be disheartening.

Anger Anger is one thing that becomes displaced because of unconscious needs and wants. A defensive response may come out when an individual fears that the other person is probably right. The expressed anger may not even relate to the current situation or conversation.

Behavior in one setting can be affected by feelings in another. And, the words communicated in any situation carry only part of the message—more spontaneous and accurate is *body language*. Look for this. Learn to read it.

EFFECTIVE COMMUNICATION

For *effective communication* to take place it must be OK to tell the truth, the whole truth, to clarify feelings and to work at dispelling misconceptions. This means sharing good things as well as things felt to be negative. If there is a communication problem, work on **why** (there is a problem)—before you work on communication skills (such as "I messages" and "feedback").

Good communication depends first on a healthy, trusting relationship. When people are reluctant to share the truth, it is usually because they don't have confidence in their own ability to handle the response. The risk is felt to be too great. But, by not telling the truth, a barrier is built. People have no *connection* with others—and thus no closeness. Honesty brings people closer because it removes barriers. To achieve this, people need to endure some periods of high emotion. And that can be frightening—as well as uncomfortable.

Response

Circumstances are only circumstances. They don't arrive evaluated. It is the response by each person that affects behavior. The response will depend on beliefs and perceptions of the situation and feelings about yourself in the relationship. If there is a conflict it may be that you each perceive the situation differently. People must clarify their perceptions of the reality before they can work on feelings and responses toward it.

Taking responsibility for feelings and responses demonstrates that people feel they have power to change the things that happen to them This confidence allows people to be more open and to communicate more honestly. Remember, learn to control things, not people.

Feelings

Feelings that affect honest communications include:
- ✓ Sense of significance (how much people feel a part of things)
- ✓ Sense of control (how they fit, how they feel in terms of competence and their level in the hierarchy)
- ✓ Sense of openness (how well-liked they feel)

When people communicate in a *descriptive* rather than *evaluative* way, the listener's response will be less defensive. It is also helpful to be specific, rather than general, in your comments. As you communicate, consider the needs of your listener and avoid comments directed at behavior or circumstances over which the listener has no control.

Feedback

Feedback is a way of giving help when an individual wants to learn how well his behavior and message match his intentions. If you are not getting feedback, chances are you are not communicating.

Feedback is most useful when the listener has asked for your feelings. Avoid imposing comments on a non-receptive ear. *Timing* is also important in successful communication. The listener must be ready to hear your comments.

Continually check with the listener to assure that your messages are being accurately received. Ask for feedback, and rephrase what you are hearing to assure accuracy.

TECHNIQUES FOR IMPROVING PERSON-TO-PERSON COMMUNICATION

The following are key points to remember in person-to-person communication:

❖ **Draw out**—Ask questions that encourage the other person to give structure to his answer. Probe fully for each explanation. Or, stop talking—this allows the other person to complete his thoughts more fully. Finally, never interrupt. This frustrates any effort to communicate.

❖ **Interpret back**—Offer your interpretation of what you have heard to test for accuracy.

❖ **Present one idea at a time**—People have a short attention span. To bombard your listener with several ideas at one time is to assure that at least some will not be remembered.

❖ **Get acceptance of one idea before moving on to the next**— Before moving to a second idea, get some assurance from your listener that your first idea has been understood.

❖ **Be explicit**—Say what you mean as precisely as possible. Generalities become ambiguous.

❖ **Be responsive to emotions**—convey an encouraging expression. Show sympathy, be reassuring and give praise.

❖ **Share your ideas and feelings**—set a trusting example.

❖ **Precede any negative comments with two points of praise**— Establish an accepting attitude in the listener so he or she will be open and receptive to your words

❖ **Work consciously on tact**—Think of how you would respond if the tables were turned.

❖ **Place yourself in the other's position**—Choose words that aren't put-downs or that imply anything negative about the listener. Your own good intentions are not enough.

Non-verbal communication carries profound messages. Body language conveys the emotional message. This is part instinctive and part learned. Be aware that these messages are being transmitted. They are usually far more accurate than verbal ones.

Inspiring Motivation

Stimulating the other person to listen is as important as transmitting ideas. The techniques for inspiring motivation have more to do with feelings and emotions than with intellect. Try to:

✤ Be responsive to emotions. Expressions of feelings are woven into the fabric of communication. They must be acknowledged through sympathizing, reassuring, praising and encouraging expressions.

✤ Give of yourself. When you share your ideas and feelings with another, he is motivated to reciprocate. Develop mutual trust.

REPETITIVE IRRITANTS

Repetitive irritants automatically turn people off. Work to eliminate these from your conversations. Remember, people don't always see their own faults although they can learn to notice. Others may not tell you that you are doing these things in words, but their body language may shout at you.

Examples:

✤ Talking to a person, through someone else

✤ Telling people, "don't worry"

✤ Topping everyone else's story

✤ Doing all the talking, dominating

✤ Calling across the room, or interrupting

✤ Not speaking up when appropriate, but complaining later

✤ Changing the subject midstream

✤ Putting someone down—especially in front of others

✤ Taking your anger out on an innocent bystander

✤ Giving people the runaround instead of straight answers

Clarity

It doesn't matter how your message sounds to you. How does it sound to your listener? To communicate successfully, begin with a content message. State briefly what you want to say; elaborate to clarify; and finally restate your key points.

Whole-part-whole: summarize your *whole* message; in more detail give the listeners each *part.* Conclude with another summary of the *whole.*

A review of Chapter 11, *Quality Management* may be helpful when speaking of communication. People cannot succeed in a project or in relaying a message if they don't define their objectives clearly. Be clear about what you are trying to do or say.

Key Points to Effective Communication

Remember to give co-workers all the information they need to proceed. But don't swamp them with unneeded information. Communication is a two-way process. Solicit feedback periodically to confirm that your message is being heard accurately.

✤ **As an effective communicator:**
  ✓ Speak clearly and loud enough
  ✓ Speak in an organized manner in a logical sequence
  ✓ Use clarifying inflection and precise words
  ✓ Speak from the diaphragm
  ✓ Look at your listener
  ✓ Speak from assurance or acknowledge that your words represent opinion
  ✓ Keep your emotions in check—express them in words ("that really makes me angry")
  ✓ Be responsive to the needs and questions of others
  ✓ Select words that have meaning to the listener
  ✓ Listen to yourself and be sure you are saying what you mean

BARRIERS TO GOOD COMMUNICATION

Even if you are conscious of and careful about all of the points above, there still may be factors that complicate good communication. These can be considered barriers to good communication. The following factors can play a part in miscommunication.

✤ Cultural differences

✤ Environmental conditions

✤ Differences in frame of reference

✤ Poor articulation

✤ Thinking faster than we can speak

✤ Evaluating the concepts, instead of listening for full meaning and implication

✤ Failure to determine from the listener how accurately you are being heard

✤ The tendency to proceed without seeking feedback from the listener

CRITERIA FOR EFFECTIVE FEEDBACK

Feedback is an essential element in effective communication. The following points can help guide you in giving good feedback.

✤ It is descriptive rather than evaluative

✤ It is specific not general

✤ It takes into account the needs of both the speaker and the receiver

✤ It focuses only on behavior that can be changed

❖ Clarification is sought

❖ It is solicited, rather than imposed

❖ It is well-timed

❖ It is based on a sincere interest in the other persons' perceptions

❖ It avoids asking *why* (other phrasing is more useful)

❖ The focus is on observations rather than references

❖ Seeks to consider elements in terms of more or less—not either/or

❖ Alternatives are explored, rather than answers or solutions

Communication is not a destination—it is a journey. A map is not the territory. A model is not the experience. The menu is not the food. People must encode ideas so as to communicate them to others. The words chosen may have a different meaning to the listener. Always check to make sure what you meant was what the others *heard*.

An effective way to communicate is to develop your thoughts with sentences that include each of the following points:

Formulating a complete thought: I *see* (documentation without judgment)
                                     I *think*—you are (not)
                                     I *feel* . . ., and,
                                     I *want* . . . (be specific)

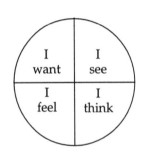

For example,
"I *see* you have missed 5 of the last 6 meetings.
I *think* we need to talk about this.
I *feel* you may not really be interested in our committee.

Develop a sentence that includes each point.   I *want* you to consider whether you need to resign."

SERIAL COMMUNICATION* Serial communication takes place when a message goes through several senders before it reaches its final destination. It is both essential and inevitable in organizations. At the same time it is very susceptible to distortion and disruption. Frequently, some of the content is omitted or added to in retelling.

❖ Details of varying importance to the transmitter become changed or dropped entirely.

❖ Details that remain are highlighted and take on increasing importance.

❖ Details become modified to conform to the transmitter's attitudes, experience, knowledge or what she expected to hear.

*Based on material by Marty Squire, Consultant (used with permission).

❖ Details are added to or exaggerated to embellish or liven up the description.

❖ Order of events is rearranged. Things are said to have happened in an order that might be expected or that seems more logical and probable to the transmitter.

❖ Statements that were originally tentative or qualified become facts, as do inferences and assumptions.

❖ Ambiguous or unclear details are adapted to make them seem more plausible or reasonable to the transmitter.

Why do these things happen? In general, as the message is passed along, each transmitter wants to make it as simple, sensible, pleasant and painless as possible. Under some circumstances, transmitters have hidden motives that lead them to make messages bigger and worse! The point to remember about serial communication is that a message never reaches the final listener in its original form. Each transmitter along the way has not just reproduced the original but has recreated it according to his needs, feelings or beliefs.

Reducing Distortion

What can be done to reduce the distortion?

❖ Make the message both written *and* oral if accuracy is required.

❖ Keep the message as short as possible. Put a minimum number of separate details in it.

❖ Keep the original message sensible and orderly and as free of ambiguities as possible.

❖ Ask the listener to repeat it to determine accuracy of reception.

❖ Anticipate any difficulties the listener may have and deal with them.

❖ Reduce the number of links in the chain.

❖ If you are the last person in the chain and the information is essential to you, go back to the original source for verification.

If you ever doubt the distortion that can result from serial communication, try the following exercise.

Prepare a single, descriptive paragraph for one individual to read to another. Ask the second individual to tell a third person what she heard and ask that person to relay the message to still a fourth. (The last two should each hear the message for the first time). What you will discover is that the last "telling" of the story differs greatly from the original paragraph. Because each listener brought a different bias and perspective to his "hearing," he colored his "telling" accordingly.

LEVELS OF COMMUNICATION
Content and Process

Communication takes place on two levels—content and process. Listen to voice tones and emphasis in the following and consider how many different things can be meant by changed inflection:

✓ *I* never said he stole the money
✓ I *never* said he stole the money
✓ I never *said* he stole the money
✓ I never said *he* stole the money
✓ I never said he *stole* the money
✓ I never said he stole the *money*

ELEMENTS OF COMMUNICATION

Real communication occurs when people listen with understanding, and this requires that clarification be sought.

When making a presentation or proposal, or planning a training or orientation session—Remember:

PEOPLE LEARN APPROXIMATELY:	PEOPLE GENERALLY REMEMBER:
1% through taste	10% of what they read
2% through touch	20% of what they hear
4% through smell	30% of what they see
10% through hearing	50% of what they hear and see
83% through sight	

If your audience retains 50% of what you present, you are a successful communicator.

BASIC WRITING

Volunteer leaders depend on the written word. It is the most used and most effective medium of communication. Writing clearly is essential. The more clearly the material is written, the better others will understand the subject being discussed.

Many times, a letter, memo or report is not understood by the recipient because it is not written clearly or does not say what the writer actually intended to say.

Five Steps

To make writing easy for the reader, consider these five basic steps:

✦ **Put each idea into one sentence.** Assuming that you have accomplished the required fact-finding, write down the essence, gist, idea or theme of what you are going to say. The sentence need not be fancy, catchy or brilliant. Writing in a simple manner is not always easy. Anyone can write complex sentences that leave the reader to sort out the facts. Short sentences are easiest to understand.

✦ **Organize your thoughts.** Keep the reader in mind. Review your writing through the eyes of the reader. Who is the reader? What are they interested in learning from you? Imagine yourself carrying on a verbal conversation with the reader. This may help you to write a message that is clear and to the point. Write as if you were talking.

Write to express thoughts, not to impress people. Clear thinking is necessary before you ever put a word on paper. Gather your material, consider the order of importance, determine the tone and *then* begin to write.

✤ **Make your writing simple.** Start out with something to arouse interest. Don't quote from someone when *you* have something worthwhile to say.

✤ **Make your writing easy for the reader**. Avoid unnecessary words. The reader may not take the time to hunt for what you are trying to say. Simplicity demands conciseness. Use short, direct, simple statements to cover basic points. Present each in a concise well-organized manner.

✤ **Avoid lengthy sentences**. Keep sentences short and to the point. Many long sentences contain several ideas. They would be better written as several short sentences. Lots of semi-colons usually means the sentences are too long.

If you are tempted to insert words such as *and, but, however* or *consequently* into the middle of a sentence, consider ending the sentence instead. Frequent use of such words may indicate that your point was not clearly made in the first place. Be economical with words.

✤ In business letters and auxiliary communications avoid timeworn, stilted phrases, such as: *this is to advise*, and *thank you in advance*.

✤ **Several common errors in writing:**
  ✓ *First annual*. If it is a first, it is not yet annual.
  ✓ *Presidents-elect*, not *president-elects*.
  ✓ The whole is *comprised* of its parts, not *composed* of its parts.
  ✓ *Demolish* and *destroy* mean to do away with completely. You can not *partially* demolish or destroy. It is redundant to write *totally* destroyed.
  ✓ Ecology and *environment* are not the same. Ecology is the study of the relationship between organisms and their environment.
  ✓ *Funeral service* is redundant. A funeral is a service.
  ✓ People don't *head up* committees; they *head* them.
  ✓ Speakers *imply*. Listeners *infer*.
  ✓ Temperatures go *higher* or *lower*, not warmer or cooler.
  ✓ Redundancies: *Easter Sunday* (Easter is enough); *Jewish Rabbi* (just Rabbi); *winter months* (just winter); *incumbent Congressman* (just Congressman).
  ✓ *Unique*— means one of a kind. Nothing can be *rather unique, almost unique, nearly unique, most unique*.

For a test of meaning consider: a foreign marketing specialist once translated back into English a popular phrase that had earlier been translated into that foreign language. The result became: "Invisible things are insane." The original? "Out of sight, out of mind!" This illustrates the point that *our* words are often just as foreign to *our listeners*. Double entendres may be impossible to grasp, such as "They'll eat that up." Make it a point to say what you mean, as clearly as possible, in terms recognizable to the listener, and without sarcasm.

Children are apt to grasp only the command in a message, rather than the admonishment "not to." "Don't touch the vase" becomes "touch the vase." As adults we may also fall into this selective hearing.

So much hinges on communication. State clearly what you expect of others in specific terms: *by what deadline* and *in what manner*. People become confused without accurate details.

ATTITUDE

Consider a group of people gathered for a fancy holiday event. Everyone is dressed in his or her finest tux and gown. When they look at the invitation they discover that the event was held last night! They break into laughter, shed their shoes and ties and decide to make their own party on the spot. There were at least two options: to become upset and exasperated because a planned event was missed (which wouldn't change anything) or to laugh it off, make the most of it and move on. This is a great example of *attitude*.

People *convey* attitudes. They affect the atmosphere by various forms of communication. Body language alone can tell others if people are disappointed or excited or angry. If people learn to intercept negative feelings before they materialize, they can assure a nicer environment for everyone.

To discuss what might have been or should have been will not change the past. Volunteer leaders have no obligation to discipline others for their failures. Maintainance of an agreeable atmosphere can convey an attitude of understanding. Fix problems, not blame.

FACE-TO-FACE COMMUNICATIONS

The following points provide a checklist of considerations to help improve face-to-face communication.

Do
- ✓ Learn to express yourself. Practice. Consider taking a speech class.
- ✓ Use your personality. Smile! Be pleasant.
- ✓ Evaluate your problems. Know why a decision was made and share the logic of this thinking.
- ✓ Consider the perspective of your listener. What is their bias and what will your words mean from their point of view?
- ✓ Rephrase your point to assure clarification if necessary.
- ✓ Speak with a voice of confidence. Remain quiet and cordial.
- ✓ Let others express themselves; allow them to differ and give them room to retreat.
- ✓ Show understanding and patience with the listener.
- ✓ Accept differences of opinions without becoming angry or upset.
- ✓ Remember, not everyone is going to agree with you. Be willing to change your position.

Don't ✓ Be bossy
           ✓ Use sarcasm
           ✓ Become angry or pout
           ✓ Take things personally
           ✓ Threaten others
           ✓ Swear
           ✓ Lose your poise
           ✓ Lose your patience
           ✓ Take a position from which you cannot deviate or retreat
           ✓ Retreat, unless of course you may be wrong

One of the factors that greatly affects communication is a person's perception of himself. Each of us enters into conversation with a picture of who we are. We try to maintain and project this picture. The listener brings to the encounter a perception of us that differs from our own. The *Johari Window* explains how this works.

JOHARI WINDOW

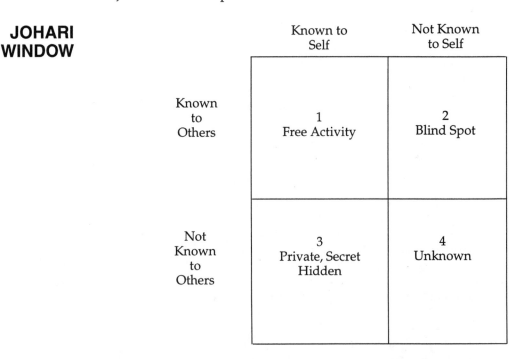

Quadrant 1: Information known to self and known to others
Quadrant 2: Information not known to self, but known to others
Quadrant 3: Information known to self, but not known to others
Quadrant 4: Information not known to self and not known to others

© 1994 Emily Kittle Morrison, *Leadership Skills*, Fisher Books, Tucson, Arizona

COMMUNICATION QUIZ

The following is a self-assessment tool. This inventory will provide you with a starting point to help develop a strategy for improving your communication skills.

Do You	Seldom 1	Usually 3	Always 5
1. Realize that what you see may differ from what others see?			
2. Realize that what people choose to say about a situation is *their* abbreviated version?			
3. Avoid labeling and using demeaning words that can destroy a person's self-esteem?			
4. Phrase your thoughts in "I" messages that describe how *you* feel about the situation?			
5. Avoid terms that imply black or white, such as *always* or *never*?			
6. Recognize that some of your words may be misinterpreted?			
7. Acknowledge that your feelings and emotions can affect what you hear, see and say?			
8. Seek to clarify your message by asking for a demonstration of understanding?			
9. Ask for feedback and clarifications when in doubt about the other person's meaning?			
10. Accept correction when it is obvious that you've been wrong?			
11. Tune into body language that might indicate misunderstanding?			
12. Avoid exaggeration and evaluation and pursue accurate understanding?			
TOTAL			

60 is a perfect score. Less than 40 indicates that you could use some work in the area of communication skills.

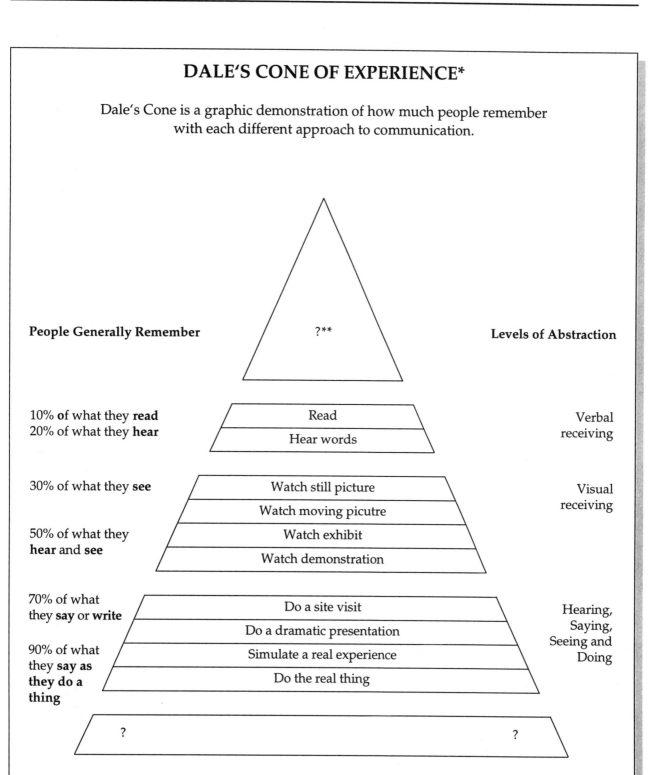

DALE'S CONE OF EXPERIENCE*

Dale's Cone is a graphic demonstration of how much people remember with each different approach to communication.

?**

People Generally Remember

Levels of Abstraction

10% of what they **read**
20% of what they **hear**

Read

Hear words

Verbal receiving

30% of what they **see**

Watch still picture

Watch moving picutre

Visual receiving

50% of what they **hear** and **see**

Watch exhibit

Watch demonstration

70% of what they **say** or **write**

Do a site visit

Do a dramatic presentation

Hearing, Saying, Seeing and Doing

90% of what they **say as they do a thing**

Simulate a real experience

Do the real thing

?   ?

* From Winman & Mierhenry, *Educational Media,* Charles Merrill, 1969, for reference to Edgar Dales Cone of Experience", used with permission.

** Question marks refer to the unknown.

8

Listening

"Do You Hear Me?"

"The reason you don't understand me, Edith, is because I'm talking to youse in English and you're listenin' to me in Dingbat!"
—Archie Bunker

It has been said that the need to be listened to is so great that if it were completely absent from daily existence, people would probably begin talking to themselves!

People need responses of all kinds. One of the most satisfying is being listened to when you want to be heard. Knowing that people care about what you have to say is important to a person's feelings of self-worth.

Beyond this, it is a comfort to know that our message has been understood. One problem that can arise is that the message sent by the speaker is not always the message received by the listener. This is due in part to the assumptions people live by:

1. Their view of how things are and what is real (what they are really like and what the world is really like).

2. Their value system (what people believe to be *good* or *bad*, *right* or *wrong* and how things *should* be).

3. How things *could* be and the possibilities for personal growth.

Connotative/ Denotative Words

Another part of the problem stems from *connotative* difficulties. The fact that different words mean different things to different people. *Denotative* or content messages—having to do with the differences in the meanings of the words themselves—can also cause problems.

Meta Messages

Dr. Paul Watzlawick has introduced still another area of potential confusion—the *meta level*. A "meta-communication" or meta message is a message about a message: posture, attitude, tone of voice and facial expression (non-verbal language). All of these affect communication and thus our listening.

People whom Maslow describes as *self-actualized* (see Chapter 6, *Motivation*) share a number of character traits. One is the acceptance of themselves and others for what they are. However, most people are in the process of *becoming* and are not fully actualized. They spend most of their energies on lower-level needs. Preoccupied with meeting these needs, people are unlikely to tune in to the needs of others and really listen.

Our school systems promote reading. This is certainly an essential skill. However, *listening* is something we are not generally taught, it is something we must learn. To learn to listen effectively, it is essential to understand the various factors involved in listening.

FIVE COMPONENTS OF GOOD LISTENING

1. Acceptance (acknowledge that you are listening)
2. Reflection (repeat the speaker's words)
3. Clarification (ask for meaning or further explanation)
4. Interpretation (absorb what has been said and reword it)
5. Summary (tie up what has been said to conclude)

Active Listening

Active listening is understanding without judging. It is more than listening to the *content* of the message. It is also trying to *understand* what is *behind* the content.

Confusion can be avoided if people rely more on a *description* of feelings. If people make a concerted effort to encourage others to express their feelings about what is happening they can expect to avoid trauma later. Unresolved feelings don't go away. They are often expressed later in a negative fashion.

Be aware that feelings may lead people to make incorrect inferences about others. It is helpful to try to understand the feelings of our co-workers. Encourage them to describe their feelings with "I" messages: "I feel used," "I feel inadequate for the job," "I feel overlooked." Send *feedback* and attempt to rephrase what was heard to see if you have absorbed the intended meaning. ("You seem upset. How would you have preferred it be handled?")

As a listener your reaction to the speaker can greatly affect communication. It is a bit unfair to say, "She is boring," when you more honestly mean, "*I* find her boring." Your own attitude plays a great part in what you say as well as what you hear.

Facial Expressions

Of all the ways a listener can encourage openness and a feeling of acceptance, the most important is facial expression. The way people say things, the tone of voice, the expression, account for about a third of what the other person perceives. I've thoroughly enjoyed working with one president because she makes my every idea sound like the best thing the group has ever considered. She does it more with expression, tone and inflection than choice of words. A person's facial expression should help communicate that she really wants to hear what the other person has to say.

Inferences Because one's behavior says so much, learn to become aware of what kinds of inferences others make from it. Remember, you will not see or hear the same events or words in precisely the same way as anyone else. Differences due to *perception, motivation, expectancies, personal bias* and such affect a person's observations and inferences.

MISCONCEPTIONS ABOUT LISTENING

There are a number of misconceptions about good listening. Among these are the idea that the ability depends largely on intelligence. And that in learning to read people will automatically learn to listen. A good listener applies specific skills acquired through training or experience. If these have not been acquired, the ability to understand and retain what is heard will be low. This can happen whether people have high or low intelligence.

While some of the skills needed for good reading apply to good listening, the assumption that one goes with the other is invalid. Listening is a very different activity than reading.

It is easier to concentrate while reading, watching or doing, than while listening. Distractions register more easily, in part because people think so much more quickly than people speak. This leaves the mind open to process hundreds of words and other factors in addition to the things we heard. The average listener remembers only 25% of what was said. Within eight hours she forgets nearly one half of that! People forget more in the first few hours than they do in the next six months.

Basic Problem The basic problem with listening is that people *think much faster than they talk*. While listening, they must receive words at an extremely slow pace compared with the ability to process. When listening, people still have spare time for *thinking*. The idea is to direct this thinking to the message being received.

To really listen, learn how to use the spare *thinking time* more effectively. Learn to direct a maximum amount of thought to the message being received. This leaves little time for mental *side-tracking* away from the speaker's message.

FOUR PRODUCTIVE LISTENING ACTIVITIES

1. Listen ahead of the speaker; prepare for the direction of thought
2. Weigh the evidence of the speaker, but withhold judgment
3. Periodically review and mentally summarize the points
4. Listen between the lines for additional meaning

Remember, facts are for constructing ideas. Grouping *ideas* is what good listening is all about. Use the *facts* only long enough to understand the ideas that are built from them.

Listening ability is also affected by emotions. Refrain from judgmental listening. Be open to new ideas or perspectives.

When possible, write down what you are hearing. Approximately 85% of what comes into the brain is through the eyes, only 11% through the ears. Taking notes can help a person to hear with more accuracy. Write down highlights and key points.

Another advantage to writing things down is that it shows the speaker that you truly care about what is being said. Once in writing, it can also be used for confirmation. "This is what I hear you saying. Is it what you meant?"

LADDER FOR SUCCESSFUL LISTENING

There are many things a person can do to become a better listener. Below is a **Ladder** for successful listening to use as a guide.

L Look at the speaker, show an active interest. (When the eyes are elsewhere so is the mind).

A Ask questions. Closed-end questions: who, what, when, where, reveal specific facts. Open-end questions draw the other person out: Why? How?

D Don't interrupt! It is as rude to step on ideas as toes.

D Don't change the subject. Interrupting is bad enough, but changing the subject compounds the error.

E Emotions. These can interfere with real communication.

R Responsiveness means being responsive to demeanor, posture, facial expression and tone of voice.

Hear For real listening, learn to **Hear**:

H *Have* a hearing check. You may not be aware of a slight hearing loss.

E *Evaluate* the evidence of the speaker for concrete support of the ideas.

A *Anticipate* the point of the communication and the direction.

R *Review* the key points mentally and summarize what you hear.

DO YOU HEAR ME?

For listening to occur there are four steps: *hearing, understanding, evaluating* and *reacting*. A good listener learns to adapt these steps into basic conversation.

Concern should also be shown for the environment in which the conversation takes place so that listening will be more effective.

Easily 80% of our volunteer activities depends on good listening. Understanding, without distortion, determines the success of various tasks, as well as the feeling generated in those with whom we work.

Listen for Concepts Listening is a process of decoding one message and reassembling it. It is based on previous knowledge. For this reason it is as important to listen for concepts, as much as for content. All words are absorbed through an emotional filter. People tend to turn off what they don't want to hear.

For this reason it is important to *market* ideas for the specific audience. Think consciously about what they want to hear and how to make each point more palatable.

Thinking and resistance drop to a minimum when people are listening to ideas that support these basic feelings. Mental barriers are dropped and everything is welcomed. Your challenge as a speaker is to create the kind of environment in which the listener will be receptive to other ideas. As a listener, tune in to your speaker with empathy and you will hear more. Time invested in the environment is worth every minute.

BLOCKS TO GOOD LISTENING

At least six factors inhibit good listening, including:

✤ Feeling that a decision must be made about what is presented

✤ Evaluating what is presented, judging

✤ Being hurried and listening on the run

✤ Hearing only what you want to hear

✤ Interrupting because you have something to say

✤ Seeing the other person as different from yourself
(in terms of group, culture, race or philosophy).

Response Styles Response styles lie at the heart of effective listening. They can act as facilitators of communication or as inhibitors. Interpersonal communication is a process of give and take. Whenever a person communicates something to you, the way you respond has the potential to direct the course of the ensuing message.

At one time or another one of the following responses may be appropriate, or at least expedient.

✤ advice-giving   ✤ reassurance

✤ interpretation   ✤ paraphrasing

✤ cross-examination

If the purpose of your communication is to share feelings then realize that the first four of these act as inhibitors. With *paraphrasing* the intention is to find out whether what you heard is what the speaker intended. This response lets the other person know you are sensitive on the *feeling* level.

THINKING STYLES

How a person listens is inevitably *affected* by his or her thinking style. William Glasser has done considerable work on the brain and how it functions as a control system. His control theory states that people are internally motivated and that behavior is always purposeful, flexible and creative. People filter situations and things through a value and feeling base. This affects how they listen and what they hear.

To understand how listening (and what is heard) can be affected, consider the following five basic thinking styles:

✦ **Affective:** This person reacts, responds, is very flexible and is open to anything, but only makes accidental connections.

✦ **Logical:** This person makes connections based on experience. Moving from details to the *big picture,* he listens for logic.

✦ **Hypothetical:** This person listens for the big picture. He makes connections by weighing questions and sorting through data which he listens for.

✦ **Rational:** This person makes abstract connections and plans carefully, listening for new ideas and options to present himself.

✦ **Adaptive:** This person is inclined to listen and respond on any of the styles above, depending on the situation.

To be a responsible, successful communicator, focus on the other person. How does he process information? Will he *listen* better if you choose words that create a picture or ones that relate to feelings? What is his thinking style? Listening improves in others when the speaker is sensitive to the values and needs of the listener, as well as his thinking style. Remember to show concern for whether he is *left-brained* (logical and analytical) or *right-brained* (creative and intuitive).

To be a responsible, successful listener, focus on the other person. Learn to empathize. Project yourself into the situation of the other person and experience the sensation believed to be a part of it. How does the other person process information. How does he *think?*

TEN COMMANDMENTS FOR GOOD LISTENING

1. **Stop talking!**
   You cannot listen if you are talking.

2. **Put the speaker at ease.**
   Help him feel that he is free to talk.

3. **Show others that you want to listen.**
   Look and act interested. Don't busy yourself with other things.
   Listen to understand, rather than to oppose.

4. **Remove distractions.**
   Don't doodle, tap or shuffle papers. Would it be quieter if you shut the door?

5. **Empathize with others.**
   Put yourself in the other's place so as to see his point of view.

6. **Be patient.**
   Allow plenty of time. Do not interrupt. Avoid heading for the door.

7. **Hold your temper.**
   An angry person gets the wrong meaning from words.

8. **Avoid arguments and criticism.**
   These put others on the defensive. They may "clam up" or become angry.
   Do not argue. Even if you win, *you lose*.

9. **Ask questions.**
   This is encouraging and shows that you are listening.
   It helps to develop points further and is essential for clarification.

10. **Stop talking!**
    This is first and last, because all the other commandments
    depend on it. You simply can not be a good listener while you are talking.

LISTENING I.Q.

This inventory provides an assessment of your current listening skills and habits.

Do You	Seldom 1	Usually 3	Always 5
1. Give the speaker your full and undivided attention?			
2. Listen for key words and underlying feelings?			
3. Avoid prejudging the value of the words until you have heard the speaker out?			
4. Wait until the speaker has completed his thought before sharing yours?			
5. Look for body-language messages as well as word messages?			
6. Steer clear of needing to have the last word?			
7. Make a conscious effort to consider and question the logic and credibility of what your hear?			
8. Ask for clarification when the words of the speaker are confusing to you?			
9. Use active listening techniques, such as paraphrasing?			
10. Attempt to remember the significant points in the speaker's message?			
TOTAL			

60 is a perfect score. Less than 40 indicates that you could use some work in listening skills.

© 1994 Emily Kittle Morrison, *Leadership Skills*, Fisher Books, Tucson, Arizona

9

Problem-Solving

"Problems, Problems, Problems"

"Fix the problem not the blame"

Life brings problems. Each day people are faced with challenges that may cause individual stress or organizational disharmony. This stems in great part from the tone set by the group leadership and the current approach used to solve problems.

Problems will never be solved until they are identified and dealt with openly. It is the group leader's responsibility to set the climate for the group, to approach problems as challenges and to make it OK to acknowledge that there is a problem. Until this is done the problem will not be solved; more likely it will perpetuate itself.

This chapter includes material on approaches to problem-solving. None of the techniques is useful until it is actually put to use by a group. To create productive solutions, those assigned to tackle problems should have certain characteristics.

Desirable Characteristics

❖ A commitment to the organization

❖ A sense of significance in the group

❖ A vested interest in finding a solution

❖ An open, creative and cooperative nature

❖ A logical, analytical mind

❖ A general sense of fairness

SIX-STEP PROCESS

Problem-solving is making a selection from a choice of alternatives. It should be thought of as a process that includes six steps:

Defining the Problem

Few problems are clear-cut. Many times the symptoms are more apparent than the causes. These symptoms offer valuable clues to underlying problems, but they are *not* the real problem.

Gathering Facts and Data

Decision-making requires that you gather all the data that might have a bearing on the problem. For the most part, this will consist of facts, opinions and assumptions obtained from observations, records or other people. If essential information is not available, delay your decision until you acquire it.

Organizing Information

If you are working with many facts or considerable data, sort out the important from the trivial. Organize the information so it can be compared and analyzed. As you study what is available, look for relationships among the various factors, such as costs, growth, schedules, advantages and disadvantages.

Alternate Solutions

Develop as many good options as possible. Quality and quantity are equally important. Most problems have more than one solution. Keep an open mind. Let your imagination roam freely over the facts you have collected. Record all possible solutions as they occur to you.

Making a Decision

Now, compare the alternatives and determine the best solution. Test the alternatives against specific criteria: the risk involved, permanency of the remedy, timing, practicality, your objectives, etc. Eliminate the unacceptable options and focus on a few acceptable alternatives. Ultimately, you will arrive at the best decision.

Evaluate the Solution

If necessary try another alternative. Be willing to work toward a true "win/win" solution. Periodic reassessment is important. Circumstances change. What would you preserve, improve or eliminate?

TECHNIQUES FOR PROBLEM-SOLVING

The following list consists of possible techniques for problem-solving. You may find one to be more effective than another. Different problems and different groups dictate which approach to use.

Systematic or Traditional

✓ State or define the problem
✓ State rules that apply, if there are any
✓ Gather/state facts that bear on the problem
✓ Propose alternate solutions
✓ Evaluate those solutions
✓ Recommend and support suggested solution, **Take Action**
✓ Evaluate—repeat process if necessary

Brainstorming

✓ Everyone involved presents ideas; these are recorded.
✓ No negative comments may be made.
✓ Ideas may be "piggy-backed." One person may enlarge on another's idea.
✓ On completion of the list, evaluate the ideas, possibly combine some.
✓ Select the best idea based upon agreed criteria. **Take Action.**

Force-Field Analysis

✓ Define the problem. Is it something you really care about? Are you personally involved? Is it possible to influence the situation?
✓ Describe it as it is now, and as you would like it to be. Restate it, indicating the direction of change.
✓ List forces that affect your situation.

Restraining Forces	Driving Forces
Forces that resist improvement	Forces which push toward improvement

✓ Review and underline two or three that seem most important right now and that you might be able to **build on.**
✓ For each Restraining Force underlined, list possible action that might reduce the effect or eliminate it.
✓ For each Driving Force underlined, list action steps that would increase the effect of each.

The place to begin to implement change is where stress and strain exist. Increased stress may be motivation for change. Keep in mind that an attempt to increase a Driving Force may result only in parallel increase in an opposing force.

✓ Review action steps and underline those that seem promising.
✓ List steps underlined. For each, list materials, people and resources available to help you carry out the action.
✓ Establish a criteria for evaluating the effectiveness of the action program. Consider the consequence of your action as well as any decision not to act.
✓ Implement your program. **Take Action**

This method requires that you describe your situation as it is now, listing the positive (what will help you) and the negative (that working against you). Then, describe it as you would like it to be. Restate it indicating the direction of change, again noting "Restraining Forces" and "Driving Forces."

The next step is where constructive, creative thinking comes in. List possible action that might reduce or eliminate the effect of each Restraining Force. Then take the Driving Forces and consider how you could increase the positive effect of each. Take charge. Become involved—don't simply become affected.

The really good thing about a Force-Field Analysis is that the group leaves with each member going off to do a job, to help make something happen or to intervene where trouble lurks.

Value Expectancy Grid

✓ Define the problem.

✓ Determine factors affecting the decision.

✓ Assign each a numerical value rating of 1-10, depending on its importance to you.

✓ Determine possible alternate solutions.

✓ Plot both on a simple graph.

✓ Evaluate those chosen factors in each of the alternatives and assign each a numerical score.

✓ Total the assigned scores and carefully evaluate the decision.

✓ Implement the plan with the highest score. **Action.**

The Value Expectancy Grid is preferred by those who are open to purely objective options.

VALUE EXPECTANCY GRID					
	FACTOR #1	FACTOR #2	FACTOR #3	FACTOR #4	FACTOR #5
1 - 10					
ALT. #1					
ALT. #2					
ALT. #3					

Problem Analysis The steps involved in problem analysis may be the simplest way to approach problem-solving. This technique requires that you:

✓ Define the problem
✓ Establish criteria—what you need to achieve, to maintain, and to avoid
✓ List criteria in order of priority
✓ Develop possible solutions
✓ Review data pertinent to solution in terms of how the data meet each criterion
✓ Test for potential satisfaction of the problem

In problem-solving, it is the job of the leader or facilitator to fully understand, without judgment, how the members of the group feel about each item discussed. She should also create an atmosphere where all ideas are viewed as worthy of consideration and have value.

Positive Imagery Analogies and metaphors are frequently helpful in generating productive ideas, as is Positive Imagery. Positive Imagery requires that you focus on what would be the best possible thing that could happen. Then work backward to figure out how to make it happen. With this approach the group should be in agreement on the "image."

As you proceed to seek solutions to identified problems, remember that each member cherishes his own individuality far more than any problem to be solved. If his individuality becomes threatened, he will not only stop cooperating but will interface with problem-solving.

Allot time for team building prior to any effort to do creative problem-solving (see pages 45-48). When all participants feel truly comfortable in the group they will become less protective of *their ideas*. They will be more willing to be objective as you progress through consideration of alternatives to selection of alternatives.

CREATIVITY A feeling of creative discontent often leads to good solutions. The discontent is what will inspire people to seek a change or propose an alternative. The creative part is hard to work with because—like motivation—it comes from within.

Cultivating Creativity Creativity must be *cultivated* within a group. To do this, it is up to the leader to:

✤ Show belief in the creative ability of the participants

✤ Help break old habits and encourage new perspectives

✤ Encourage innovation

✤ Suspend premature judgment

✤ Protect members from feeling foolish

✤ Avoid criticism of individuals or their ideas

✤ Discourage negative comments

✤ Steer away from competitiveness within

✤ Loosen rigid thinking

✤ Bring confusion into focus

Pre-plan Results

If you pre-plan for results, you will find that what looks like a problem will solve itself. Outlining the expected results puts you on a path toward success.

It is also helpful to break routine. If routine approaches are coming in conflict with desired results, change the routine. For example, if fewer and fewer members seem to be attending your 9 a.m. meetings, try meeting at lunch, or in the evening or on Saturday. Find some time that produces a greater success ratio. (If in fact it is the *hour* that is the problem and not some other factor).

Logic

Logic, the ability to be quantitative, analytical and verbal and to conceptualize freely and think creatively are all useful traits in problem-solving. This includes the ability to *identify* the problem. If the problem is not properly identified, it will not be properly solved. This stems from the tendency to spend too little effort on *problem definition* so as to get on with problem-solving.

Most problem-solving is approached with fear and trepidation—if not a sense of crisis. Life is full of problems. Each day brings new problems. However, it is more productive to view each as a *challenge*. When talking about group or committee problems, be systematic in your approach.

Few people like problems. As a result, there is a tendency to pick the first solutions that comes to mind. This may lead to worse problems than existed before.

If you proceed to change your meeting time, having decided people aren't coming because of the hour, you may still have a low attendance. In fact, they may not be coming because they had expected great programs and you no longer provide them. Part of the solution may be found in simply *listening* to what your members are saying.

It would be a great if problem-solving was an exact science, but acknowledging that it is not is the first step in the solution. A second is to recognize that a major stumbling block to problem-solving is the failure to first identify and agree upon the *criteria* for an acceptable solution. Once these are delineated, potential solutions can be weighed objectively.

✤ What do you want to achieve?

✤ What must you preserve?

✤ What do you seek to avoid?

✤ What has more priority?

And, a third step is to remind all concerned that the solution will be only as good as the information considered. Analytical minds will not create practical and productive solutions if their discussions are based on inaccurate or inadequate information.

FOUR LEVELS OF INFORMATION

Be conscious of the kind of information you are considering. Your solutions are only as good as the information on which they are based. There are four levels of information to consider when gathering data:

✦ **Fact:** That which has actual existence

✦ **Inference:** A logical conclusion based on fact

✦ **Speculation:** A theory based on conjecture rather than fact

✦ **Opinion:** A belief stronger than an impression

Opinion and Fact

The material that is identified as *opinion* is generally too subjective to be useful in problem-solving. The aim should be to gather all the *facts*, pertinent and available—and to make decisions based on that information.

Wise Decision-Making

To make a wise decision:

✦ Know where you want to go

✦ Know what has to be accomplished

✦ Know the alternate ways to get there, and weigh them

Problem-solving is often tackled in a general brainstorming approach, with no focus. The problem as stated may be too big and beyond reach. To be realistic about it, divide the problem into manageable components.

A useful technique to help focus is to ask "why," and to keep asking "why" until you finally arrive at your real concern. "How can we build a better mouse trap?" is a fine statement. If you ask "why," you discover you really mean "What is the best way to catch mice?," or even "How can we rid our homes of mice?," or "How can we keep our homes free of mice?" Each Problem Statement opens up a different focus and thus a different solution.

Before attempting to solve to a problem be sure you have identified the problem and not merely a *symptom* of the problem. When you have, state it as a question.

The Problem Analysis Chart on page 125 is designed to help you focus on the real nature of your problem and to communicate with others your perception of the situation. You can chart your information in a useful manner by filling this out with a small group assigned to develop a proposed solution. It allows you to test each of your criteria against the possible solutions.

For everyone to "buy into" the chosen solution, those affected must be given the opportunity to be *heard*. Everyone comes from a different set of priorities and experiences. Their willingness to help the solution work will depend on their investment in the selection of that solution. "Bottoms up is the bottom line." Listen to the ideas and feelings of those affected by the solution.

In creative problem-solving, avoid thinking in absolutes and consider ideas on a spectrum from *really good* to *very bad*. Each consideration can then be placed, with consensus of the group, somewhere on the spectrum.

REALLY GOOD ◀━━━━▶ VERY BAD

Synergism   Synergism is also a great term to keep in mind when approaching a problem: "Mutually reinforcing action of separate agents or ideas which together produce an effect greater than that of all the components acting separately." I can think of some solutions. You can think of some solutions. But together, by sharing our ideas, we will create more than the total of your ideas and my ideas. Together we can build on all the ideas for still other, better ideas.

Any of the approaches listed can be successful. The situation will determine which is best. In any case a conscious approach, rather than a haphazard, crisis approach, will assure the selection of a successful solution.

The best way to produce change is to come up with an alternative that everyone prefers to whatever is happening now. To encourage positive, creative thinking within your group, begin by asking that people come to you with possible solutions rather than problems. This gives people the feeling you trust them to identify their problems and have faith in their ability to generate potential solutions.

Always respect the individuals more than the structure. *Listen.* Remember that for someone to win, (by having his solution selected) someone else need not lose. The best solution will benefit everyone.

Encourage Cooperation   As a leader or chairman you need not feel it is your responsibility to make all judgments, solve all problems and hand out all edicts. Rather, it is up to you to help your co-workers spot problems and work together to devise alternatives and seek solutions. In problem-solving, *cooperation* should be encouraged and competition discouraged.

The chairman or leader who brings an attitude of cheerfulness, understanding and cooperation to each situation will find his co-workers reflecting these characteristics in return.

A good chairman will seek to develop a sense of confident respect for himself and others. He will show an appreciation for individuals and their differences. If we don't respect our committee workers, we can hardly expect them to demonstrate respect for us or our project. People need to appreciate the worth of others.

It is difficult to see a problem from the point of view of others. However, it is an essential consideration in conceptualizing, and it leads to a better solution. This is because it takes into consideration the many interests of others. The solution will be acted upon more readily if it represents the expressed feelings of all affected.

The ability to see a problem from another person's point of view is the key to successful problem-solving. Gain a feeling for the viewpoint of others so as to achieve an acceptable solution. Always ask yourself how others might be viewing the issue, from what bias and from what value base. If in doubt—**ask!**

BLOCKS TO PROBLEM-SOLVING*
Perceptual Blocks

✚ *Difficulty in isolating the problem:* Is the meeting-attendance problem one of when it is held?, or maybe what is offered?, or where it is held, or even who is handling it? Weigh *all* of the possibilities.

✚ *Tendency to limit the problem area too closely:* Have you failed to consider peripheral aspects of the situation? Some things at first glance may not appear to be related to the problem.

✚ *Inability to see the problem from various points of view:* Have you taken the time to consider how each of the others involved might view the situation?

✚ *Seeing what you expect to see:* (Stereotyping) Have you tried altering your focus or changing your point of view? Try painting a portrait from a photo turned upside down. You will see what is there—not what you expect to be there.

✚ *Saturation:* Many extremely familiar things are not recorded in our memories in ways that allow easy recall. Can you identify the letters that go with the numbers on your phone . . . without looking?

✚ *Failure to utilize all sensory input:* Our senses are interconnected—taste becomes inhibited when smell is suppressed. In reverse—sight is augmented by supplementary sound.

Cultural Blocks

We also suffer from Cultural, Environmental and Emotional Blocks. Cultural blocks are those that bring judgment into play. This judgment is generally confining and responsible for squelching creativity. Among the most common cultural blocks are the ideas that:

✚ Logic, reason, practicality, utility are *good*; pleasure, feelings, qualitative judgments are *bad*.

✚ Fantasy and reflection are a waste of time.

*Adapted from material by James L. Adams in *Conceptual Blockbusting, a Guide to Better Ideas,* with permission of the author and the publisher, W.W. Norton & Co., Inc., N. Y., N Y. Copyright 1974, 1976, 1979 by James L. Adams.

❖ Playfulness is childish.

❖ Problem-Solving is serious business; humor has no place in it.

❖ Tradition is preferable to change.

❖ Any problem can be solved by scientific thinking and lots of money.

❖ Taboos.

Unless people are aware of these they may hinder efforts to solve problems. There is considerable evidence that suggests fantasy, reflection and mental playfulness are *essential* to creative thinking and productive conceptualization. Unfortunately, these properties are frequently "socialized" out of people after childhood. Unless people are lucky enough to work with others who encourage creativity and reward innovative ideas, they are apt to be stifled. Creative problem-solving is less likely to take place.

Environmental Blocks   The area in which ideas are considered can affect the outcome. A number of elements are included in terms of environmental blocks, such as:

❖ Autocratic leaders who value only their own ideas and fail to reward others

❖ A lack of cooperation and trust among co-workers

❖ Lack of support that would bring ideas to action

❖ Distractions such as telephones and other intrusions

The ability to conceptualize requires that a combination of previously unrelated structures be seen in a new way, incorporating logic and reason with intuition and feeling.

Motivation is essential in creativity. Unless those involved truly want to solve the problem and see that they will be affected by the effort in a positive way, they will probably bring little enthusiasm to the task.

Therefore, it is essential that those ultimately challenged to work out a possible solution (based on input from everyone affected) be those in your group who bring the greatest interest and motivation to the task. Unless a member is truly convinced that a change is needed, he is not likely to *see* ways to bring about a change.

I can't stress enough the importance of support. Non-supportive responses, especially from a chairman or other authority figures, are very harmful to creative problem-solving. Most people are at least somewhat unsure of the quality of their own ideas. They require a supportive environment in which to work.

An atmosphere of honesty, trust and support is absolutely necessary if people are going to be encouraged to be creative in designing solutions. A friendly, non-competitive, interactive climate can help to encourage people to generate new ideas and to have the courage to express them. For these reasons, a chairman must praise and reward all the participants for their efforts on a regular basis.

As if Environmental, Perceptual and Cultural Blocks were not enough to stand in our way of problem-solving, we also face *Emotional Blocks.*

Emotional Blocks Emotional blocks relate to factors of confidence and self-esteem. They are a result, in part, of who we are temperamentally. Some people have a:

- ✤ Fear of failure

- ✤ Need for order and security (inability to tolerate ambiguity)

- ✤ Preference for judging ideas, rather than generating them

- ✤ Lack of challenge (no motivation)

- ✤ Inability to relax and incubate ideas

- ✤ Lack of imagination

- ✤ Excessive zeal; eagerness to succeed too quickly

- ✤ Inability to distinguish reality from fantasy

- ✤ Lack of imaginative control

- ✤ Need to feel they are right

Most people have been rewarded for *right* answers and punished for mistakes. A sense of *failure* makes people feel they let others down. A leader's challenge is to provide a non-judgmental environment (so all ideas are given consideration) where people are allowed to generate options different from the norm.

Tolerance for Ambiguity Fear of making mistakes is rooted in insecurity. Such insecurities are responsible for the inability to tolerate ambiguity. Finding the solution to a complex problem can be a messy process. In a sense, problem-solving is bringing order out of chaos. The ability to tolerate some chaos seems to be necessary to creative thinking and productive problem-solving.

Compulsive people who must always have everything in its place seem less able to work with certain types of problems. The process of bringing widely differing thoughts together cannot take place in a mind that will not allow incompatible thoughts to exist together long enough to combine.

People are all affected to a greater or lesser extent by each of the blocks cited above—*emotional, environmental, perceptual* and *cultural*. Effective leaders are aware of these and deal with the effects. The best people for creative problem-solving are those who can be objective and who are less affected by the blocks discussed.

If you foresee annual or perpetual problem-solving sessions, it is probably time to provide training in problem-solving skills. Such training can increase members' awareness of typical blocks to problem-solving and the need to work around them.

People can not be expected to change their behavior or approaches if they are unaware of alternate ways. They must be able to recognize any weakness in their current styles.

Ask Dumb Questions

Creativity requires the manipulation and recombination of experience. The creative person needs the opportunity to fantasize freely and vividly. One of the most important abilities of a creative person is a questioning attitude. Unfortunately, many adults resist asking questions because it is an admission of ignorance. Again, constructive discontent is productive.

Dumb questions are easier to handle than dumb mistakes!

People have nothing to lose and a great deal to gain by questioning. By questioning things, people can also look at situations from new angles. Try adapting, modifying, magnifying, minifying, combining, rearranging and reversing.

Exercise your own mind. Begin to apply some of these strategies. Stretch your mind to begin to hold many ideas at one time—in some confusion— and allow these to germinate and to interplay with all others. This will help you to become better at problem-solving.

CHECKLIST FOR NEW IDEAS*

The following checklist can be applied to avoid being trapped by one of the blocks. It is great for *innovation*, rather than *evaluation*.

Modify

New twist? Change meaning, color, motion, sound, odor, form, shape? Other changes?

Magnify

What to add? More time? Greater frequency? Stronger? Higher? Longer? Thicker? Extra value? Plus ingredient? Duplicate? Multiply? Exaggerate?

Minify

What to subtract? Smaller? Condense? Miniature? Lower? Shorter? Lighter? Omit? Streamline? Split up? Understate?

Adapt

What else is like this? What other ideas does this suggest? Does the past offer a parallel? What could I copy? Whom could I emulate?

Reverse

Transpose positive and negative? How about opposites? Turn it backwards? Turn it upside down? Reverse roles? Change shoes? Turn tables? Turn the other cheek?

*Adapted from *Applied Imagination* by Alex Osborn with the permission of Charles Scribner's Sons, © 1953, 1957, 1963 by Charles Scribner's Sons; © 1981 by Russell Osborn.

Put to Other Uses New ways to use as is? Other uses if modified?

Rearrange Interchange components? Other pattern? Other layout? Other sequence? Change pace? Change schedule? Transpose cause and effect?

Substitute Who else instead? What else instead? Other material? Other ingredient, other process? Other place? Other approach? Other power? Other tone of voice?

Combine How about a blend, an alloy, an assortment, an ensemble? Combine units? Combine purposes? Combine ideas? Combine appeals?

These ideas need not apply simply to products in the business world, but can be used to consider projects and fund-raisers which have always been profitable but perhaps need a new angle.

PROBLEM-SOLVING PROBLEMS* The following is a list of reasons why your group may be limited in its ability to solve a particular problem or problems. Refer to this list to help identify specific areas that need attention. Remember that a *process* is only as effective as the *people* who are using it.

✤ **Personal and Interpersonal Attitudes and Behavior**
   ✓ Individual needs for identity, recognition and security
   ✓ Severely competitive behavior
   ✓ Need to dominate others
   ✓ Overly defensive behavior
   ✓ Inaccurate interpersonal perceptions (one member may think another is threatening)
   ✓ Lack of attraction by the group for some members
   ✓ Unreasonable conformity to group pressures
   ✓ Poor communication

✤ **Identification of the problem**
   ✓ Lack of mutual concern or lack of any concern
   ✓ Lack of cohesiveness in the group regarding the problem
   ✓ Inability to overcome confusion

✤ **Definition of the Problem**
   ✓ Failure to compare what is, with what is desired
   ✓ Inability to agree on the scope of the problem
   ✓ Inability to agree on the severity of the problem
   ✓ Lack of factual information (too much reliance on unverified opinions and guesses)

✤ **Generation and Selection of Solutions**
   ✓ Lack of identification of possible solutions (inexperience in the area or lack of creative thinking)

*Adapted from *Problem-Solving and Group Interaction* by Bobby R. Patton and Kim Giffin, Harper and Row, NY, 1973. (used with permission).

✓ Poor identification of criteria for evaluating solutions
✓ Inability to agree on a group decision

❖ **Implementation of Group Decision**
✓ Inability to sort and allocate resources
✓ Inability to agree upon individual members' responsibilities
✓ Inability to persuade others to give support and approval

❖ **Role Functions**
✓ Inability to agree on who is to perform leadership functions
✓ Poor match between member's temperament or skill and the role requirements

❖ **Group Characteristics**
✓ Group is too large or too small
✓ Poor cohesiveness
✓ Lack of status or prestige of the group
✓ Unacceptable group norms (such as tardiness and absenteeism)
✓ Ongoing power struggle
✓ Lack of individual commitment
✓ General apathy

❖ **Conflict Within the Group**
✓ Inability to discriminate between honest disagreement and interpersonal difficulties
✓ Inability to be comfortable with honest, reasonable disagreement

❖ **Selection of Appropriate Discussion Modes**
✓ Inability to choose alternate formats for group thinking (such as brainstorming, leaderless discussion, sub-groupings, committees)
✓ Inability to structure discussions
✓ Too much leader dominance of discussion

One of the wonderfully naive things about most people is the belief that simply by forming a committee or establishing a Task Force any problem can be solved. It just isn't so. Too often we must actually settle for the best option available. And it may not truly be a solution.

All problems do not have solutions, per se. However, this is not to say people should stop looking or become resigned to troubles that spring eternal. Just identifying the existence of a problem puts us closer to a solution than before it was openly acknowledged.

The following form is for use in sessions with groups interested in identifying their problems, developing criteria for success and in generating possible solutions.

© 1994 Emily Kittle Morrison, *Leadership Skills*, Fisher Books, Tucson, Arizona

PROBLEM ANALYSIS CHART
(for Decision-Making)

1. **DEFINE THE PROBLEM:** _____

2. **SPECIFY CRITERIA:** (What we want to do)

   ACHIEVE: _____

   PRESERVE: _____

   AVOID: _____

3. **ESTABLISH PRIORITIES:**
   (Give a numerical value to the importance of each criteria.)
   1 = essential
   5 = least important

   3.
   _____
   _____
   _____
   _____
   _____
   _____

4. **DEVELOP POSSIBLE SOLUTIONS:** (Identify ways to solve the problem considering the identified criteria.)

   A. _____

   B. _____

   C. _____

   D. _____

   6.

5. **SPECIFY DATA:**
   (What do we know about each solution as to how it meets the criteria.)

   A. _____

   B. _____

   C. _____

   D. _____

6. **TEST:** Look at each possible solution and consider how well each meets our criteria and priorities. Give a number value to each solution. 1 = very effective 5 = least effective

7. **SELECT ONE:** _____

10

Time Management

"It's About Time"

Time management is really much easier to discuss in a workshop than a handbook. This is because what we value, what priorities we hold and how we use our time greatly affect our *view* of time.

There are national seminar leaders who promote the idea of "working smarter" to assure more productive use of your time, and helping others to do the same. To me, this really means simply being *aware* of what you are doing with your time. It will slip away if you don't plan for the careful use of the hours you do have.

HOW TO MANAGE YOUR TIME

If you don't manage your time, it will be managed for you. It will be scheduled and stolen by others who need you. The hours for all those things you wished you had accomplished will have evaporated. Set goals for yourself and share these with others.

Planning

The real key to success here is in doing some *planning*. Set some specific objectives. What do you want to accomplish? By when? If you don't say it, or state it, it is not likely to ever happen. Make a commitment to goals in general and objectives specifically.

The list makers of the world are on the right track because they at least have set out *to do something*. They may not have concluded that some things are more important than others, but they know what they would like to do. And that is a start.

127

One of the first things to remember when planning your time or simply wondering, "Where does my time go?" is that *your value system greatly affects the way you use your time.*

Value System

If you value harmony you may spend a considerable part of your day acting as an arbitrator in an attempt to keep the peace. If you value praise, you may put your greatest energies into those things that will be noticed by others. If you value neatness, may spend your day straightening and organizing *things*.

Because we all value different things, it is important to recognize and acknowledge these differences, especially in those with whom we live and work. It is also important to communicate our feelings with others—if we want their cooperation in maintaining a certain standard. We can't presume that others feel as we do or that they even know how we feel.

Equally important is the fact that some things are not valued at all. When conflict arises over things we hold as important, problems can certainly be expected. Two areas come quickly to mind—time and money.

As we work in the community with others, we soon find that there are some who:

1. would rather invest their money than give of their time.
2. would rather give of their time than invest any money.
3. do not place too much consideration on the money involved. This can mean *your money* for such things as sitters or material goods.
4. seem to have considerable time to waste—those who don't seem to pre-plan events. As a result, everyone's time is unwisely spent.

VALUE OF TIME

If you begin to value time, you'll invest it wisely. In my workshops I always have the participants think for a minute about the idea that *their time is worth money.* What if you were given $1,440 every day—and told if you didn't spend it that day, you would have to return it? Every day you would be given another $1,440. How would you spend it? This is how many minutes you will find in each day and if you haven't invested them—you have lost them. You can't come back tomorrow and say, "You know the two hours that slipped away yesterday afternoon? I need them today."

TIME INVESTMENT

Time invested in the *process* of living is as important as the tangible, measurable things. Good relationships don't just happen, they take *time* and pay great rewards. Don't diminish the value of things you can't measure. To sit on the porch and watch the sun go down may seem unproductive to some—but if it leaves you rejuvenated and ready to give your all to a project, then it is time well spent. If it brings you closer to those dear to you, or helps you to understand someone you work with, it is time well spent. We all value different things. Because of this, we will invest our time differently.

TIME PRIORITIES

If you are aggravated with yourself for wasting time, perhaps you have never taken the time to set down specifically what you want to accomplish. Make lists. Be reasonable. You will only assure disappointment if your list is unrealistic. Keeping a calendar for commitments helps you to balance time and build realiability. Schedule time for yourself and your projects.

Once you know what you want to do, you can then consider how you want to go about accomplishing these things. A check list, in order, can save back-tracking. It can also be helpful in deciding on priorities.

"What is the best use of my time *right now?*" is a question you should ask yourself often. By remaining flexible, you can shift from one project to another, depending on the interferences which complicate a typical day. Carrying something with you to do if you must wait for others can give you a feeling of accomplishment and reduce stress. Answer neglected letters, catch up on leisure reading. Make a list of "Things To Do." Invest your time in productive activity.

BLOCKS OF TIME

One real key to accomplishing a great deal is the use of *small blocks of time.* Some people seem to say, "There really isn't time to start anything." It is better to look at situations as *found time.* Be aware of the many things you face that can be done a little at a time. Keep these things handy. Close your door if you need uninterrupted time. Place a small orange flag on your pencil jar and tell co-workers you are very busy when the flag is up. Ask them to please wait to interrupt until the flag is down.

DELEGATING

The next major time saver is *delegating.* To save time acknowledge that there is no way you can do everything. Do the things you want to do most. Delegate some tasks to people around you. It builds responsibility and encourages consideration. (see page 66)

Of course, it is time lost if the individual assigned is unable or fails to accomplish the assigned task, to your satisfaction. Here are a few rules for delegating:

✤ **Choose** people capable of handling the job.

✤ **Clarify** your expectations; they should be clearly understood.

✤ **Believe** in the individual's ability to carry out the task.

✤ **Commit** the individual to the promise of following through.

✤ **Set deadlines** and stick to them.

❖ **Allow lattitude** and encourage initiative.

❖ **Follow up**—keep on top of the assignment.

❖ **Don't do it** for them.

❖ **Reward** the individual in keeping with the results produced.

TIME-WASTERS   One of the primary reasons we don't accomplish all we would like to is that we allow time-wasters to steal our precious hours and minutes. Each of the following factors contribute to wasting time.

Procrastination   A notorious time-waster. By setting a time limit, a deadline for yourself, with specific goals, you will be less likely to procrastinate. You might also reward yourself when you have finished a task. Or, try doing the worst jobs first.

Misunderstandings   When receiving or giving assignments, make a supreme effort to assure yourself that everyone involved fully understands. If things aren't done right the first time, when will you have time to do them over? (see Chapter 7, *Communication*)

Interruptions   If you need to work in isolation, go to the neighborhood library. If you have things to do at home, but the telephone persists in ringing—turn it off! A note on the door can politely discourage interruptions. Schedule your activities so you will be alone when quiet is needed. When you can deal with interruptions, do things that aren't affected by having others around.

Lack of Preparation   Plan before meeting with others. Know what points you need to cover and what answers you want—and expect the same of them. Let others know you are busy and it is important to you that they give things some advance thought. Mentally walk yourself through events to establish what needs you will face with the actual situation.

Perfection   reduces your productivity rate. Give frank consideration to just how important perfection is to each task facing you. Extreme perfection is an unrealistic use of time. This is not to suggest that you compromise your standards—just be realistic. It doesn't mean settling for the mediocre.

Clutter   If you can't find it, you lose considerable time searching. "A place for everything and everything in its place"—is ideal, including the wastebasket! Must you save everything? Set up a personal file box with folders for such things as Bank, Car, Utilities, House, Taxes, School, Club. If it works at the office it will probably work at home.

Lack of Energy Unless you invest some time in your own good health—eating right, exercising, getting enough sleep—then you will have fewer hours to count on.

Decisions If too many basic decisions require your attention, you lose time. Help others to develop the ability to make decisions. Make decisions at the lowest level possible. Ask others to bring solutions to you, not problems. Ask how they would solve the problem.

There are really no shortcuts. Time management doesn't happen without effort. You must be aware of how much time you have and how you want to use it. Invest a little time in planning ahead to save time in the end.

HELPFUL HINTS FOR TIME MANAGEMENT

To find those extra hours needed, to fulfill yourself as a volunteer in a community which reminds you that you are needed, you are appreciated, you are special, you may have to shift your priorities a little. Consider:

- Have something constructive to do with small blocks of time.

- Keep "busy work" activities near the phone (things that need action but not attention)

- Anticipate—when shopping, load up (potential gifts, especially children's, future birthday cards, frequently used items such as soap and toothpaste). Plan your trips to town in a logical order.

- Invest in a 25-foot-long telephone cord that will provide you with mobility while on the phone (better yet, get a cordless phone!)

- When bogged down—move on; go to something else.

- When practical do two things at once—change a bed while doing a load of laundry.

- Have people bring you possible solutions rather than problems.

- Set specific, realistic objectives to be accomplished each day.

- Keep your long-range goals in mind while doing your smallest task.

- Clarify, don't waste time because of misunderstood instructions.

- Make a realistic estimate of your time available; don't set yourself up for failure.

- Set priorities and plan for the best time to accomplish the most important tasks.

- Learn to say "No," and don't feel guilty when you do.

- Select the best time of day for the type of work required.

✦ Build on success and don't waste time regretting failures.

✦ Think positively about the success of your goal, whatever it is.

✦ Help those around you to develop a sense of independence and faith in themselves.

✦ Make decisions at the lowest level possible. Train others to make decisions without you.

✦ Remember that time spent organizing and planning pays off in time saved later.

✦ Do it now!

✦ Approach projects as a collection of small tasks rather than one over-whelming challenge.

✦ Make specific lists of things to do today—check them off.

✦ Don't allow others to steal your time. Explain that you are busy, and get on with *your* projects.

✦ Learn who can handle responsibility. Delegate often.

✦ Continually ask yourself, "Am I making the best use of my time right now?"

PERSONAL TIME LOG

DATE	BUSINESS OR VOLUNTEER RELATED						PERSONAL					KEEP HANDY FOR RECORDING
GOALS 1. 2. 3. 4. 5. 6.	ROUTINE WORK	COMMUNICATION	TELEPHONE	PLANNING	ACTION & DECISIONS	OUTSIDE ACTIVITIES	PHYSICAL HEALTH	FAMILY	LEISURE ACTIVITIES	PERSONAL GROWTH	OTHER	NOTES, COMMENTS ON OPPORTUNITIES FOR IMPROVEMENT
6:00 a.m.												
6:30												
7:00												
7:30												
8:00												
8:30												
9:00												
9:30												
10:00												
10:30												
11:00												
11:30												
12:00 p.m.												
12:30												
1:00												
1:30												
2:00												
2:30												
3:00												
3:30												
4:00												
4:30												
5:00												
5:30												
6:00 p.m.												
6:30												
7:00												
7:30												
8:00												
8:30												
9:00												
9:30												
10:00												
10:30												
11:00												
TOTAL HOURS												

Keep a record for a week of the amount of time spent in each area.
Make comments to yourself about how you might improve the situation.

© 1994 Emily Kittle Morrison, *Leadership Skills*, Fisher Books, Tucson, Arizona

Quality Management

"In the Beginning . . ."

"In business the competition will bite you if you keep running;
if you stand still they will swallow you."

S. E. Knudsen

MEASUREMENT OF RESULTS

Managing a business—even a non-profit business—demands concern for *how* the agency or organization does what it does, as well as *what* it does. Management generally refers to concern for the 'tasks' to be accomplished. However, for total quality management to be the norm, there is an investment in the people who *do* the tasks. There is a sense of *team* involvement.

Clarify Purpose and Goals

For your organization to succeed, consideration should be shown for the following:

✤ Shared values and vision

✤ A clear mission (goal) and focus

✤ Well-defined objectives (with time uses)

✤ An atmosphere that promotes risk-taking

✤ A climate of empowerment

✤ A shared enthusiasm for the challenge

✤ A sense of appreciation felt by all

✤ A nurturing environment

✤ An attitude of flexibility

✤ An awareness of the community climate

✤ A regular review of progress

Each of the points listed above is an essential concern for any organization truly interested in succeeding. Without a clear mission and focus, both staff and volunteers will be at a loss to understand the goal and direction of the organization. Establishing goals and spelling out objectives is what once provided the basis of MBO—Management by Objectives. The concept remains valid.

Managing with goals and objectives provides a yardstick to measure the results of projects or programs. It is a credible method for determining how well organizations and agencies have achieved their mission. It is also a systematic way to plan that anticipates positive results. It is measurable structure where new ideas can be drafted. It is the blueprint for the future that allows the 'laborers' to be working toward the same end—to be building an agreed-upon success.

This system helps groups to clarify their purpose and goals. It allows members to identify achievable objectives that demonstrate how they will measure the results. It helps groups to focus energy —something 'visualized' by everyone. The 'picture' of success is clearly agreed upon.

Accountability is essential for incorporated non-profit agencies to maintain a tax-exempt status. And it is also necessary if organizations are to convince donors (individual, corporate and foundation) that their's is a worthy cause.

There is considerable competition for dollars and donors. In each case the demand will be made to, "Show me why I should donate to *your* agency, over ABC's?"

Because agencies are 'non-profit' there is a misconception that there is no real need for money or manpower management, or accountability. But there is! To survive, not-for-profit organizations must become every bit as effective and accountable as commercial businesses.

Non-profit organizations, like any organization, need a mission and purpose, as well as specific objectives to achieve. These objectives relate to delivering the highest quality service possible with a realistic expenditure of time, energy and money. Managers and Boards of non-profit agencies have a responsibility to utilize any available assets in a prudent manner and to be accountable for results.

Initiating an approach based on objective setting requires considerable pre-planning and effort. Failure to invest this time and to develop a clear-cut set of objectives, however, invites potential problems and may perpetuate crisis management.

INITIAL CONSIDERATIONS

To set up an organized approach to management in your organization, begin by setting a specific time for each subgroup, division or committee to consider:

✓ What is our mission or purpose?

✓ What Key Result Areas do we want to address?

✓ What realistic goals can be established?

✓ What reasonable, measurable objectives could be proposed? (Remember, the plan, approach or strategy should be developed by those responsible for the outcome).

✓ What time frames should be attached to each objective?

✓ Whom could we assign the authority to for making this happen?

✓ How will we measure progress toward each objective?

✓ Who will be responsible for evaluating the success? By when?

KEY RESULT AREAS

The first consideration, before setting goals or establishing objectives, is that of identifying "Key Results Areas." Dale McConkey goes into depth about this in his book *How to Manage by Results*.

As with the process of actually establishing objectives, this takes time. But it will save time and frustration in the long run. Set a meeting with your planning committee and devote it to identifying "Key Results Areas." These are areas of consideration in which it is absolutely essential that a high level of performance be assured. These are matters of highest priority. The purpose is to help the chairman or executive director to direct the limited resources (i.e., money, manpower, materials, time and authority) in a manner where the greatest return is assured. Identify what is truly important *before* writing objectives.

Think in positive terms. Identity results sought.

✤ **Results**—not procedures

✤ **Results**—not the process

✤ **Results**—not the activities

✤ **What**—not how

✤ **Ends**—not means

✤ **Output**—not input

Ultimate Accomplishments

With "Key Result" considerations the focus is on *ultimate accomplishments*. When ideas are listed they usually fall into one or more of four general categories:

✓ quantity

✓ quality

✓ cost

✓ timeliness

One word of caution: avoid considering any *measurement*. This is premature at this stage. As with problem-solving, suspend judgment

How to Manage by Results, 3rd edition, by Dale McConkey, AMACOM, NY, © 1977.

during your first phase. Measurements should be specified in your objectives. At this stage you are interested in *identifying* subject matter. Your concern needs to be in selecting the areas where the highest level of performance is essential.

Remember to address the issue of the effectiveness and satisfaction of your staff and volunteers. Surely one 'Key Result' area should focus on these issues. For 'Total Quality Management' there is a demonstrable investment in *people* and the *process,* as well as the mission and related tasks. Staff and volunteers are actively involved in establishing direction and evaluating results.

S.W.O.T. — SITUATIONAL ANALYSIS

After you have identified your Key Result Areas, analyze your capability to actually achieve a high level of performance. Employ a S.W.O.T. analysis.

Identity what advantages you can expect with this project. These are *strengths* and *opportunities.* Anticipation of disadvantages is also important. These are *weaknesses* and *threats.* Each of your Key Results Areas should be analyzed for Strengths, Weaknesses, Opportunities and Threats. The first two are concerned with the present. The second two are geared toward the future.

✦ **Strengths**—advantages operating in a favorable manner on which you should capitalize.

✦ **Weaknesses**—disadvantages which will impede performance and must be hurdled.

✦ **Opportunities**—future advantages which should be used to your best ability.

✦ **Threats**—future happenings or changes that may have a significant impact on your success. An attempt should be made to minimize these.

A careful S.W.O.T. analysis should help you to identify focus areas for your objectives and provide a guide as to the level of achievement you can realistically expect. It can also help you to set priorities.

Examples

An example of S.W.O.T. Analysis for a hypothetical group might be:

✦ **Key Result Area**   A full staff of volunteers for all identified positions

✦ **Strengths**   Excellent facility
Convenient location

✦ **Weaknesses**   No public transportation
Greatest need: late-night volunteers

✦ **Opportunities**   A growing community
Nearby college with internship needs

✦ **Threats**   Other local social service agencies in the building draw from the same volunteer pool
More and more volunteers are getting paid jobs

Behavioral scientists have noted that man is very capable of self-direction and control in reaching objectives . . . *if* they are things to which he is committed. Individuals are willing to accept, and even seek responsibility under encouraging conditions. Establishing an accepting and trusting environment in which ideas and solutions can flourish is one of the challenges of volunteer leadership.

It is worth the effort to contact a local resource person to provide training and consultation in advance of this session, or to facilitate an objective-setting session with you. Organizations currently using such an approach may have volunteers willing to work with you. Consider calling such groups as the Junior League, the United Way, the Red Cross and the Y.

Each of these have strong training components. Local colleges or universities may have someone on staff willing to help you. Sometimes people from from the Service Corps of Retired Senior Executives (SCORE) or Small Business Administration are willing to help. There are also nationally qualified trainers (such as your author) who deal exclusively with non-profit organizations in the realm of volunteer and board training.

If this all sounds overwhelming and confusing, it may be because it is new to you. As with Interaction Recording, try it—you'll like it. I promise. *Any* pre-planning you can do pays off in the long run. It may seem like time you can't find. But if you fail to invest it in the beginning, you'll pay for it later.

OBJECTIVE SETTING One of the major pitfalls for many volunteer groups is their failure to clearly spell out:
- ✓ what they want to accomplish
- ✓ by what date
- ✓ how they can measure this.

Frequently the suggestion is—"Let's have a Walkathon! We've done it every year. Who can we get to do it this year?" With turnover what it is, you will probably discover that last year's coordinator moved to Podunk and took all his expertise with him . . . in his head.

If you are luckier than many, he turned in a one-page report that listed all of those who helped and maybe a little about how it was publicized and how many prizes were presented. Oh, and the fact that they made $3,120 for the agency.

But wouldn't it have been helpful to know that it took all year, burned out a dozen volunteers, cost $7,500 to produce, was too hot in the middle of July, and that the staff did most of the work? Call the previous coordinator long-distance and find out as much as you can about what happened. Get him to tell you what he feels happened and what could have happened with certain changes.

You' will never know whether it is time well spent if you don't set clear objectives before you start. Do you want to make money? How much money? Use volunteers? How many? Is having fun important? Involving the Board? A well thought-out proposal in advance of the "how to's," will include the allocation of basic resources: money, manpower, materials, time and authority.

Make sure you have stated your objectives so well that a totally uninvolved person would find them absolutely clear, with no surprises or presumed areas of understanding. *Nothing* goes without saying. Spell out your expectations in the beginning.

This is important in committee or Board work of any kind. To assure an interested, enthusiastic group, clearly spell out the requirements of each position and expectations concerning meetings, attendance, preparation, participation, involvement. By the same token, group members have a right to know what they can expect in terms of clarification, support, and encouragement.

The challenge to every volunteer leader is to gain skill in dealing effectively with tasks as well as people. Learn to be a positive goal-oriented manager, while being sensitive to the people who make things happen. In other words, become an Executive. A volunteer executive is no different than a business executive. He has a responsibility to his agency or organization as well as to the people who staff it, volunteer and paid.

THE MANAGEMENT PROCESS
Management vs. Leadership

There is a distinct difference between Management and Leadership, although the words are often used synonymously. Leadership deals with motivating people to achieve a goal. It is concerned with only one commodity—people, their needs and emotions. Management deals with organizing resources in a specific, intelligent manner to achieve goals effectively. The primary emphasis is on getting results. A comparison of management versus leadership will show the difference.

MANAGEMENT	LEADERSHIP
essentially intellectual	essentially emotional
appointive office with	elective with power
power from the people	from above
stable	temporary: leadership rotates
analytical/problem-solving	function of empathy
focuses on results	focuses on people
a science, concerned with task	an art, creative/innovative
rewarded by achievement	rewarded by personal
and results	relationships

Management is a problem-solving system based in logic. Effectiveness as managers is predicated on a willingness to discipline yourself to adhere to the system, processes and controls of the science. Some lucky souls are Executives by nature and are fully qualified and skilled at leading as well as managing.

An Executive

Goal-oriented	Decides
Thoughtful	Uses staff work
Results-oriented	Directs
Effective	Mediates
Long-term planner	Represents organization
Mission-oriented	Sees whole
Attracts talent	Operates in internal and
Works in future	and external politics
Manages resources	Synthesizes
Studies environment	Concept-oriented

AN ANALYTICAL SYSTEM

The management process is nothing more than an analytical system of organizing resources to get results. It can be learned through study and discipline. It takes a lot of practice to do it well, but the rewards are enormous. The chief advantage is that it forces you to verbalize *exactly* what it is you want to do before you jump into planning and doing the job.

Use of the Management Process

✤ Assures that programs and projects will be well managed and plans continued, despite turnover in personnel

✤ Increases enthusiasm
   ✓ members have advance knowledge of what is expected
   ✓ members are involved in overall planning and determination of standards used in evaluating performance
   ✓ emphasis is on results rather than methods employed in achieving them—encourages innovation
   ✓ achievements are easily measured

✤ Requires planning; minimizes crisis management

✤ Provides clear, mutual understanding on matters of procedure

✤ Gives members a sense of direction and security; knowledge of where they are, where they are going, and why

✤ Operates with a minimum of lost or wasted effort or resources

✤ Builds in future planning, due to cyclical nature

✤ Is adaptable in personal, voluntary and business life

OBJECTIVES

The most difficult job in management is translating an organization's goals and its general statements of intent into defined and specific objectives before initiating any planning or tackling any job. Such objectives must direct activity. They should contain specific figures and standards that are meaningful to the people whose progress and results are to be measured. A group has a clearly defined and communicated objective when every one involved can answer:

✤ What will be different or achieved upon completion?

✤ What is the time limit?

✤ How will the difference be measured?

Where are objectives set? The Board of Directors should set organizational objectives. Staff and committee chairmen should establish objectives and plans to meet these Board and organizational objectives.

Organizational objectives are more complex to set than personal ones, because organizations by nature encompass the aspirations and efforts of many. Some objectives are quite properly in the domain of one committee, some the obligation of the whole organization.

Many committee objectives are limiting ones, offering strategies (how something will be accomplished) as part of the objective. Board objectives should never include any *strategy* in the statement of what will be different. Many times objectives are not fulfilled in one year. In some cases different people will be carrying them out (as tends to happen with a rotating Board). However, this is the beauty of the management process. It is designed for future planning. Each year builds on the previous one.

It is important that objectives be realistic. If they are not realistically attainable, they will only produce frustration. If, on the other hand, they are too easily reached, then there is no challenge and they will not move the organization forward.

Specifying objectives at the outset ensures that the entire organization, committee or Board knows what it is trying to do. It enables decisions, policies and priorities to be made in the light of what the group is trying to accomplish.

PLAN OF ACTION

Once you have a clear objective with a time frame and measurement, planning involves walking through the experience *backward*. You know *what* you want to have happen at the other end. So *how* are you going to make it happen? Planning a blueprint is necessary to achieve your objectives. Inherent in any good plan are four basic considerations:

1. Decide what overall strategy the group will use to accomplish the task.

2. Allocate the various resources as needed.

3. Establish a monitoring system to warn of impending failure.

4. Formulate alternate plans for use when the control system indicates performance is not meeting expectation.

Stragegy

Strategy is nothing more than a statement as to *how* the plan will be achieved. Several strategies may fit the objective. The group must decide on the one(s) on which it will collectively focus organizational efforts.

Resources

You have five *resources* available. These form the checklist by which a plan can be reviewed for completeness, effectiveness and thorough understanding.

Manpower—How many people do you need? Who will select them? Who will do what? What training do they need? Who will coordinate their efforts?

Money—How much do you have? How much do you really need? Where could you get more? Where could you cut? How will it be allocated? Accounted for?

Materials—What do you need? How will they be selected? Allocated? Maintained? Produced? Accounted for?

Time—How much do you have? How much do you need? Do you have a reserve? Is there a critical time frame on which the plan hinges?

Authority—Who has it? How should it be divided and delegated? How many restraints do you have from others?

CONTROLS

The most successful managers are those who have not only thought about what might go wrong, but have actually established the warning system that will tell them in time to do something about it. This is not to say they *expect* to fail, rather that they are *prepared* to deal with complications. They have a Plan B. (If Plan B does not work, remember there are 24 more letters in the alphabet!)

Controls should be established with input from the group. In this way everyone in the group has a clear picture of what is wanted and what is expected. It develops a feeling of security and pride because everyone knows where he stands in relation to the total "game plan." Every individual must know precisely the extent of his responsibility, the scope of his authority, the standard of performance expected and the resources available. He must be *asked*, not told.

Typical Controls

✤ **Standards of performance**
These establish the expectations so variations can be detected. They consist primarily of time schedules, job descriptions and budgets. They provide built-in guides and protection for the individual. They reveal progress toward interim goals; an opportunity to make corrections before it is too late; and give the satisfaction of knowing you are on the right track.

✤ **Feedback**
This is a method of reporting that is basically unstructured. It consists of meetings, oral and written reports and confirmation letters. It is founded more on a *feelings* reaction than an intellectual assessment.

✤ **Personal observation**
The more a manager can personally observe the situation, the easier and earlier adjustment can be made in the plan, if it becomes necessary.

ALTERNATE PLANS

All items judged to be both serious and likely should be examined to see what form of alternate planning will produce adequate protection at a reasonable cost. These alternate plans will then be ready to go into effect when your control system shows that performance is not meeting expectations.

The basic rule is: the easier it is to recover from something going wrong, the simpler your alternate planning need be. Look for the aspects that really make a difference. Make your detailed alternatives for those. No plan should be considered complete until it has been tested for possible failure and alternate plans have been incorporated.

THE PROCESS The first two steps of the management process are essentially the planning steps. Step three is the doing step, the one in which the entire organization is involved. Management's role turns from one of planning to one of active direction and supervision.

The key to effective execution is well-qualified and motivated people. Leadership, rather than management, determines the group's dedication to effort. At this point active vigilance and flexibility are essential. Allow freedom and trust to those responsible for the accomplishment of each task. Establish an atmosphere of enthusiasm.

Remember—one of the greatest advantages of a management process is its emphasis on *what* is to be accomplished rather than on *how* a job is to be done. There must be ample room for individual initiative and innovation within clearly defined work boundaries. This is communicated in the controlling step of planning. These controls must be relatively broad and designed to show deviations from set plans rather than interfere with detailed actions of subordinates.

APPRAISAL Appraisal is the systematic analysis of all factors that make an organization effective in achieving its objectives. It lays the groundwork for setting new objectives and can be considered a first step as well as a last step. It is a critical tool to ensure that the group builds each year on its past successes—that it formulates new goals and objectives. This establishes a constant record of accomplishment.

There are two types of appraisal: internal and external. An external appraisal is basically looking outside the organization at all the community factors that might affect the internal planning and execution. Such factors might include available funding, other community efforts, the economic picture, service needs, etc.

An internal appraisal is comprised of three basic elements:

Results Did you meet your objective?

Resources What were your results versus resources expended?

Management Did the management work for you?

One failure on the part of many leaders is the tendency to assess only the negative. Successful groups are built out of assets, not liabilities. Thus a good management appraisal requires a balanced assessment. Review strengths as well as weaknesses, successes as well as failures, the positive as well as the negative.

Criticizing only what has failed or is going wrong, presents a very warped view of reality. This leads management into spending a disproportionate amount of time trying to straighten out problem areas instead of capitalizing on those resources that are proving effective.

Results
The first element to appraise is the *results*. If the objective has been clearly defined and communicated, the group will continuously assess its position. But there should always be a final appraisal at the conclusion of the year or event. This becomes an occasion for rewards and group satisfaction. Consider whether your original objectives were met.

When considering resources, look at the results compared with the resources expended. Appraise each of your five resources (3 M's, T-A), *money, manpower, materials, time* and *authority,* and evaluate whether each was well utilized. Could you have done the job with less money or would it have been better with more? In achieving the objective, did you burn out the chairman, under-utilize the committee or rely too heavily on one person? Were your materials adequate? Did you have enough? Too little? Did you have enough time or was the time expended not worth the result? Did you have difficulty delegating authority?

Appraisal of Management
In appraising your own leadership, go back through the four steps of the management process and evaluate each, for both the positive and the negative. Was the objective clearly defined and communicated to the entire group? Was the objective well stated with a good standard of measurement? Was the objective realistic? Did you have difficulty planning the action? Was the strategy well stated and were the resources realistically allocated? How well did your controls work? Were you adequately warned of possible failure? Did everything proceed on schedule? Did you have difficulty knowing when to step in? Did you have an alternate plan? Was it well developed? Did you need it? This is a self-appraisal of how well you managed.

If a group or committee systematically assesses past performance against the criteria of *results, resources* and *management,* the strengths and weaknesses, problems and opportunities will quickly become apparent. This will allow you to develop new, realistic goals. These can be translated into definitive, measurable objectives—and thus begin the planning and operating cycle once again. Transitions will be easy and the group can continue independent of the individual members and their respective roles.

P.I.E. EVALUATION
The P.I.E. Evaluation form is designed to evaluate the effectiveness of a project or program by considering each of the resources involved (Money, Manpower, Materials, Time and Authority) from an objective standpoint. Members of the group responsible for the activity should be convened soon after completion and asked to consider each resource in terms of whether the approach should be Preserved ("It was perfect!"), Improved ("Good, but next time I'd . . ."), or Eliminated ("Let's not *ever* . . . again!").

Following the appraisal the group is then set with new directions and future planning can evolve from the successes of the past year. Objectives can then be created by an outgoing committee and given to an incoming committee. The new group is then in a position to begin the cycle all over again—setting new objectives based on the suggestions from the previous group.

P.I.E. EVALUATION FORM			
	PRESERVE	**IMPROVE**	**ELIMINATE**
MONEY			
MANPOWER			
MATERIALS			
TIME			
AUTHORITY			

MANAGEMENT OVERVIEW

"Never mistake motion for action."
—Ernest Hemingway

An effective manager identifies Key Result Areas and proceeds to specify goals and objectives. For each objective a concept is briefly described and resources allocated, on paper. The manager develops these with co-workers who will be involved. Realistic alternate plans are specified and controls established.

Process

Effective management depends on a recognition of the importance of the *approach* as well as the goals and the people. It is a *process* orientation and a commitment to continuity and communication, with clarification that yields success. It is the result of time and effort being invested in the beginning.

This approach forces you to verbalize what you want to do *before* you jump into planning or are actually doing the job. It ensures that programs continue despite yearly turnover, and that everyone understands clearly what is planned.

Goals

Open-ended statements of hopes for the group or committee.

Objectives

Specific and measurable. Objectives have three parts:

1. What will be different or accomplished?
2. By when?
3. How measured? Each objective should relate to at least one goal.
   ✓ **Words to use**—to write, to identify, to solve, to compare, to contrast, to improve, to conduct, to develop, to communicate, to establish, to obtain, to increase, etc.
   ✓ **Words to avoid**— to know, to be aware, to understand, to appreciate, to believe, to educate (too nonspecific).

Objectives do **not** state *how* you are going to accomplish something but instead, *what* you will accomplish.

Organize For Action   How are you going to accomplish your objective?

There can be more than one plan of action. The plan is called your *concept* (or Strategy). State this briefly, only after you and your group have agreed on the objectives.

Plan Resources   To develop any plan or strategy, you will have five resources to consider. These include:

- ✓ **Money** (budget)
- ✓ **Manpower** (who will be needed for every aspect of plan)
- ✓ **Material** (tangible things needed)
- ✓ **Time needed** (schedule of activities)
- ✓ **Authority** (who is responsible for each component)

Alternate Plan   Be sure to have an alternate plan. If cancelation is not an option, invest time and energy developing a plan that can be put into motion if needed.

Establish Controls   This is a check system *established at the outset* to let you know that everything is going as planned. To do this:

- ✤ **Set standards of performance:** Make sure each member knows what is expected of him, what quality is acceptable and the time schedule to be followed.

- ✤ **Provide avenues for feedback:** Oral or written, such as progress report at a Board or committee meeting.

- ✤ **Personal observation:** Chairman should be available for support and assistance at subcommittee meetings.

Execute the Task   Combine good management with good leadership. Be sensitive to the feelings of the members and their needs, but be strong by being a good manager backed up by a good plan.

Appraise   This can be the end of the objective or the beginning of another objective.

- ✤ Did you accomplish what you set out to do?

- ✤ Were your resources used effectively or not?

- ✤ Did you follow the management process well? (If not, why not?)

- ✤ Are you pleased with the results?

- ✤ What would you **P**reserve, **I**mprove and **E**liminate?

© 1994 Emily Kittle Morrison, *Leadership Skills*, Fisher Books, Tucson, Arizona

THE MANAGEMENT PROCESS

GOAL (open-ended) _____

OBJECTIVE (alterable)
What different?_____
By when? _____
How measured? _____

CONCEPT
(strategy) _____
_____
_____

ORGANIZE FOR ACTION
(allocation of resources)
1. Money:_____
_____

2. Manpower: _____
_____

3. Material _____
_____

4. Time _____
_____

5. Authority_____

ALTERNATE PLAN (plan) _____
ESTABLISH CONTROLS
(strategies for observation-feedback-reporting out)
_____
_____
_____
_____

EXECUTE THE PLAN (do it!)
APPRAISE (evaluate)
1. Did you achieve your objective? _____
_____
2. Were your resources allocated properly? _____
3. Was the management process used? _____
4. Recommendations for future action _____
_____
_____

(Duplicate form for each separate objective)

12

Conflict Management

"Let's not fight about this"

In the interest of harmony, people often push aside conflict and ask members simply to be considerate, or perhaps to try to be understanding. It is the reaction people fear. Strong opinions, threatened egos, strained relationships and a lack of objectivity can make people uncomfortable.

Discomfort and Emotion
When you become open and direct about conflict, situations can become uncomfortable. However, without it there will be a cold war. At some point you must decide whether to deal with the discomfort of the conflict indefinitely, or to endure a temporary state of high emotion (and considerable discomfort) while you and your members address the basis of the conflict.

Many view it as a sign of weakness to abandon their stand. What is needed is an attempt to help the individual to look at things in a different way. Help the person to change her perspective and ultimately her attitude. Always pave the way for a graceful retreat so the individual may maintain a feeling of self-respect, if compromised.

Rational Opposition
Rational opposition can usually be countered with facts. However, before trying to change the bias of others be very sure that your own position is based on solid facts. What may actually be at issue could be differing *values*. Where this is the case, acknowledgment will clear the air, but it is unlikely that the conflict will be resolved.

Irrational Opposition

When dealing with irrational opposition, first express appreciation for the other person's feelings on the subject. Be understanding of the *feelings,* if not their rationale. A person may resist change without being aware of it.

Then describe the problem or area of conflict, as you see it. Is this how the other person views the situation? Seek to come to an agreement of what the problem is. Your conflict may only be perceptual.

FUNCTIONS OF CONFLICT

All resistance and conflict need not be seen as negative. Each can serve a very useful function. It can:

✤ Cause the leader to clarify more sharply the purpose of any proposed change and the results sought.

✤ Point out the need for a greater sense of 'team' within the group itself.

✤ Disclose the inadequacy of the current problem-solving or decision-making techniques.

✤ Bring to light the weakness in the communication process and the flow of information.

Diagnosing Conflict

To diagnose conflict, identify the nature of the difference.

✤ **Is the disagreement based on:**
   ✓ facts?   ✓ goals?
   ✓ values?   ✓ methods?

✤ **Identify the underlying differences**
   ✓ Is the individual influenced by his role?
   ✓ Does the individual have access to all the information?
   ✓ Does he have a different perspective of the same information?

TASK vs. PROCESS

It is regrettable that most of our dealings within organizations, or affiliations with Boards, are approached from the standpoint of a *task* to be accomplished. Having a common interest (the blind, the museum, the Scouts, the school), is important. Allow time for consideration of *process* as it will affect the results.

It is necessary to invest energies in making things happen. Recognize that the outcome and feelings of satisfaction will be affected by the *process* involved in making it happen. If everyone is in perpetual conflict you may still reap thousands of dollars. But along the way you may lose many reliable and productive members, because of of frustration and discontent.

CONFLICT MANAGEMENT

To minimize resistance and conflict there are several things a volunteer, particularly a volunteer leader, can do. Here are five points to consider.

✤ Think consciously about your problem-solving technique

✤ Maximize the participation of your members in all decisions

✤ Encourage imagination and creativity

✤ Open up communication by helping everyone to feel at ease

✤ Keep an open flow of information

**MANAGING
CONFLICT**

To *manage* conflict be willing to alter your approach to dealing with conflict. To do this, first identify how you are currently handling conflict. Do you:

✤ **Complain**—or do you suggest reasonable change?

✤ **Shut out others**—or do you ask for and give feedback on conflict issues?

✤ **Stand by your guns**—or are you willing to consider compromise?

✤ **Make presumptions about other people's positions**—or do you seek clarification?

✤ **Label people**—or do you stick to the issues instead of the personalities?

✤ **Continually cite what happened last week, last month or last year**—or do you concentrate on what is happening now?

Recognizing that your own current behavior may worsen the problem puts you in a position to rethink your approach. Remember—**the only person you can change is yourself.** However, by changing your actions, you can create a new *climate* and ultimately a new *reaction.*

**BARRIERS TO
CONFRONTATION**

Many times conflict is not openly dealt with because the parties involved find that *excuses not to* deal with it outweigh *reasons* for confrontation. Individuals are reluctant to leave their *comfort zone,* even though it may mean solving the problem. It involves *risk-taking,* which is a scary thing for many people.

Some of the barriers to open confrontation include:

✤ Insufficient time to work things out

✤ Feeling that volunteers, especially chairmen, should not express negative feelings

✤ Personal concept of your role within the group

✤ Public image concerns

✤ Desire to avoid hurting others' feelings

✤ Fear of your own vulnerability to the other's conflict tactics

✤ Fear that your efforts will not be reciprocated

Once you have considered these barriers and have recognized the need to make a change in yourself (or to take a stand or risk) you are then in a position to manage conflict. Conflict really shouldn't be avoided; it should be acknowledged and where possible, resolved.

STRATEGIES   A difference of opinion need not be viewed as a conflict area. *Perception* decides whether or not there is a conflict. When you decide there is in fact a conflict, there are at least five identifiable strategies for dealing with it:

Competition   Useful in emergencies, when an unpopular decision has to be implemented.

Avoidance   Useful when you perceive it is best to leave well enough alone, to buy time and when damage caused by confrontation will outweigh benefits.

Accommodation   Use when the issue means more to others, when harmony is seen as more important, when you are open to a solution other than your own.

Compromise   Use to achieve a temporary settlement, when time is of the essence, when you are working from mutually exclusive goals.

Collaboration   Problem-Solving. Use when concerns are too great to compromise, when solution affects long-range trends, when the decision will greatly affect all involved.

Instead of *choosing* a conflict-management strategy, people most often respond in a typical style. Some are very competitive, others are accommodators. Some are avoiders while others are always driven to find a compromise—or at least to collaborate.

PROBLEM-SOLVING   Problem-Solving is the most permanent way of dealing with conflict. It takes the most effort and requires the cooperation of all. It involves an approach that can lead to a win/win solution. The steps include:

1. **Diagnosis** of the kind of conflict

2. **Initiation** of a confrontation
   ✓ Identify the tangible effects the conflict has
   ✓ Avoid putting the participants on the defensive
   ✓ Criticize only the situation, never the people

3. **Active Listening**
   ✓ Hear the other's point of view
   ✓ Clarify by restating the view of others to assure your understanding
   ✓ Have regard for the feelings and words of others

4. **Problem-Solving** itself is the final step, begun only when all agree there is a situation (a problem) that needs change

For suggestions about productive and effective problem solving see Chapter 9, *Problem-Solving*.

NEGOTIATING

"Knowledge is the skill to take something apart. Wisdom is the ability to put it back together again."

If conflict management is a *skill*, negotiation is a *fine art*. For example, if your group is faced with negotiating for a percentage of the profit from a commercial booth at a local fair, send your best negotiator. Some of us are simply too willing to accept *any* offer. Others are capable of working out an arrangement that is still acceptable to all involved—and may be better than the first offer.

With this in mind, the following points are important in negotiating. Your awareness of these will put you ahead from the start.

- ✤ **People are different**—they have different needs and they perceive things differently. Present your case in a manner that relates to the others' needs.

- ✤ **Make things personal**—of course you are representing your organization or group, but make the point that you are counting on this individual.

- ✤ **Negotiate privately**—don't set out to accomplish change in a public situation where an individual is apt to be more concerned with defending his stand or saving face.

- ✤ **Propose an ultimatum**—only if you are in a position to back it up (such as never renting their facility again) and if the other party believes you will back it up.

- ✤ **Deal face to face**—it is easier to say "no" on the phone or in a letter. Don't give your opposition this advantage.

- ✤ **Always initiate any call or meeting**—*you* have the advantage of coming prepared and setting the terms, including the ultimate deadline.

- ✤ **Always initiate the contract or memo**—*you* establish the terms.

- ✤ **Never hesitate to ask for help**—from the opposition, to understand or to clarify. Get them involved in a collaborative effort and attempt to diminish the competitiveness of the environment.

- ✤ **Consider timing**—look for the best time, not just any time, to negotiate. This can affect your prospect for success.

- ✤ **There are always options.** Make the choice. You be the one in charge of the situation.

When negotiating, your influence is related to the extent to which you share open communication, as well as the degree of trust established. The relationships people have within a group can greatly affect not only their actual power and influence, but how much they are perceived to have. For this reason, a healthy organization will invest in developing trust among its members. This process should begin early in the association of any group.

Obstacles to effective negotiation are reduced considerably if concern has been demonstrated for each member as an individual, and by keeping open the doors of communication.

The fact is that to effectively negotiate with dissenters your first concern should be with the inter-personal relationships. Unless people are willing to let down their guards—and at the same time feel safe and unintimidated—they are in no position to negotiate differences objectively.

Communication skills and a warm, caring feeling of team are primary elements in an effective organization or Board. Once these have been established, a group is in a position to set about *negotiating*.

Competencies   Competencies important to negotiating and influencing others include:

❖ A degree of personal security (poise and confidence)

❖ Situational skill (ability to perceive complexities)

❖ Independence and courage of judgment (ability to substantiate claims, and stand strongly for a position)

❖ Ability to abstract and conceptualize

❖ Mental flexibility (ability to adjust and to add new dimensions)

❖ Tolerance for ambiguity (not pressured to find immediate solutions)

❖ Ability to analyze and synthesize (to see relationships)

A quick glance at the list above will tell you why you may occasionally fail at your efforts to influence change. To affect change, the parties involved *must have* the needed skills to negotiate.

Regrettably, many of the difficulties faced by non-profit agencies revolve around inner turmoil and ineffective inter-personal relationships. This simply points to the need to be as concerned about *how* you do what you do as you are with *what* you do.

Considerable effort should be invested in the *process*. An annual orientation of group members can establish the tone for the year. If it is approached in a positive, constructive, organized manner the message will be, "We want to work with you, we care about you, we're glad you care about us."

Then, if and when any problems develop, you are in a far better position to persuade. A win/win solution is possible, but only when an atmosphere of understanding and caring has been established. Organizations can only be effective when they devote as much attention to the process as to the products of their efforts.

PREPARATION FOR NEGOTIATION

Essential considerations when approaching a negotiating situation include:

+ Know what you want
+ Be prepared with facts
+ Know what your opposition is
+ Prepare your presentation, point by point
+ Anticipate reactions
+ Develop an approach in tune with the other's capacity to understand and appreciate
+ Develop a climate of cooperation
+ Remain open to the feelings of the other
+ Help the other to develop a better position
+ Allow the other to save face
+ Steer away from an approach that will incite defense mechanisms
+ Demonstrate concern for the other's self-esteem
+ Consider timing and method

STEPS IN NEGOTIATING

To be an effective negotiator, learn to listen to what the other person wants and needs, and appeal to these. Welcome objections, and show appreciation for the other person's point of view (even if you do not agree).

Step 1 Phrase your proposal in such a way as to assure agreement to several points at the beginning. ("I think we can both agree there is a problem, and something really must be done," for example).

Step 2 Seek to remove obstacles to agreement by developing a sense of progress. ("It seems to me we both agree that x, y, z.")

Step 3 Create a common sense of flexibility and appreciation for the other person's efforts. ("I appreciate that you see my point here, and I agree that x,y,z.)

KEYS TO EFFECTIVE NEGOTIATION

Whenever there seems to be a need to negotiate with co-workers or other community people there are several key points to remember. The following will help assure the ultimate satisfaction by both parties:

+ Remain open to the other's point of view
+ Avoid overselling
+ Stand strong in your position (don't apologize for it)
+ Let the buck stop here
+ Exercise patience

❖ Be gracious and courteous

❖ Emphasize the positive

❖ Avoid arrogance, belittling, ridicule and sarcasm

If it would be helpful, the points listed above could be reviewed by the parties involved just prior to entering into the negotiating process. This chart could be kept at the table or on the wall for reference to assure that each is approaching the situation on workable terms.

"Criticism is like surgery. It always hurts and at times it can be fatal. It requires careful preparation by both physician and patient. The doctor must be calm and steady, and the patient must be willing and ready."
　　　　　　　　　　　　　　　　　　　—Dr. Haim Ginott

Dr. Haim Ginott recommended that we learn to respond, instead of to react. This is very hard to do when emotions are high and trouble brewing. However, when we react we are reflecting our own experiences and feelings. We are behaving because of what *we* know. Taking time to respond calmly allows you to relate to the other person's feelings.

Conflict should neither be welcomed nor avoided. It is to be expected. Conflict is bound to occur in any group of people with great concern for issues. Conflict reminds us that we are human. Solutions are only possible when conflict is acknowledged and dealt with openly, with the help of all concerned. It is a challenge, a hurdle, but it need not be an insurmountable barrier to success.

Confronting Issues

The ability to confront (specific issues) depends on several factors:

❖ A sense of significance in the relationship

❖ An interest in saving the relationship

❖ A feeling of self-worth

❖ A belief that you will be *heard*

❖ A clear idea of how you 'feel' and what you want

❖ Knowledge that the other person cares about changing things

❖ An open, honest, trusting base

❖ A commitment to something greater than the two individuals

If any of the above points are not established it is an indication that this item must first be dealt with and discussed. Without a healthy relationship, confrontation simply ignites defenses and encourages anger.

Avoiding Confrontation

A few reasons why people *avoid* confrontation include:

✤ **I don't want to hurt the other person.**
The intent is to make things better. Sometimes it hurts to hear that we are not doing what we think we are (see page 99). But this hurt allows for the possibility of finding a solution. Pain is our 'reset' button.

✤ **If you can't say anything nice you shouldn't say anything at all.**
If said in private, and with the interest in making things better, it ought to be said.

✤ **I'll just sound like a nag.**
A nag speaks only of the problem. In effective confrontation a solution is proposed or negotiated.

✤ **I don 't want the other person mad at me.**
The truth hurts and sometimes makes people mad. Be sure to deal first with creating a climate in which emotions are calm.

✤ **Nothing will change.**
As long as you believe it won't, it won't. Change your attitude and it just may. The only way to find out is to try. It surely won't if you don't bring up the issue.

13

Self-Assessment/ Group Assessment

"Where Are We Going?"

"It is your attitude, not your aptitude, which determines your altitude."

Make your life an adventure in which you are proud of your role. Have a goal. And periodically evaluate your adventure. Stay on course and give yourself both an opportunity to avoid pitfalls and a chance for personal praise. It is just as important that *you* view what you are doing as productive and positive, as to be recognized by others for this. Take time to evaluate your progress; reward yourself. By doing this, you will strengthen your identity and be less vulnerable to the effects of invalid criticism by others.

This may require simply a change in perspective. Try altering your view of those things that you conceive as problems. If seen as challenges, they take on a whole new light. Remember that yesterday is behind you. I hope you learned from it—but don't dwell on it and don't let it get you down. Work on today. Live now! This is your only chance to experience this moment. Why not make the very most of it. Live it to the fullest. Let all senses be alive.

"The quality, not the longevity, of one's life is what is important."

Develop a mental picture of the person you would like to be. It's the first step in becoming that person. Focus your efforts on activities within your area of competence. Consider what your strengths are and

159

what exceeds your ability. Be honest and realistic. Also, choose tasks that are not in conflict with your values or you're apt to find unhappiness ahead.

GETTING TO KNOW YOURSELF

The picture you get of yourself is from the responses others have. If you choose to ignore these, you have learned nothing. But if you take note, you are ahead. For example, do you find you are never elected to office but perpetually appointed "chairman of the world?" Perhaps it is because you are a manager rather than a leader. There is a difference, and knowing the difference can set you on the track of a more satisfying path.

Leaders are born, but *leadership* can be learned. Leaders are people with a sensitivity to others, who recognize feelings and respond from emotions. Many positions are absolutely perfect for a person like this, including right hand to a chairman. They can serve as a buffer, much as they work well in vice-presidential slots. They can temper tensions and emotions between personalities.

Leaders are those wonderful people with charisma who inspire others by the smiles on their face or the twinkle in their eyes. They are the Pied Pipers of the world. With positive factors working on their side, they turn out to be the John F. Kennedys of the world instead of the Sadam Husseins. They are *elected* to positions of authority.

Managers, on the other hand, are those appointed to office. They are recognized by others as having considerable skill and ability in dealing with tasks. They have analytical problem-solving minds and work from intellect —what the facts tell them.

The skills of management can also be learned. Leaders can learn to become good managers by applying tools that help facilitate the process of accomplishing tasks. Unfortunately, it is much harder to learn to become a leader, but not impossible. It involves learning to be sensitive to others. It presumes a sincere interest in others.

Science and Art

Management can be seen as a science, one of getting things done by allocating resources, with the focus on results. Leadership is the art of stimulating (motivating) people to do things. The focus is on the people.

As volunteers you can take an objective look at yourself and say, "My title may be Girl Scout *leader*, but I am really much more of a manager. I am a task-oriented person." Acknowledging this, seek to work at a level and in an area where such skills are essential. Let those with a greater sensitivity to people handle those positions that require leadership skills.

The concept of "Flying up" with a Scout troop is potentially as irrational as the Peter Principle in business: "In a hierarchy every employee tends to rise to his level of incompetence." As long as you are performing magnificently as a Brownie leader (planning, organizing, executing) why move up to Junior Scouts? This is where a sensitivity to the girls' needs and abilities is far more important. Opportunities for planning and organizing should be passed on to the girls. It may frustrate you if the job isn't accomplished to your satisfaction. But it may frustrate the scouts if you continue to do *for* them and offer few opportunities for them to learn to plan and organize for themselves.

This is not to say that you could not do both. Just take a minute to appraise yourself, to assess your skills, abilities and temperament. Are you equally capable of this opportunity as you were the last? Moving in is not always moving up if the requirements of the job are alien to your abilities. By the same token, for some, being overall chairman—orchestrating the activities of others—may be far easier than the responsibilities of a single committee chairmanship, if it is the wrong one.

Volunteering should be fun. It should leave you with good feelings. There is a flexibility in terms of time commitment and requirements not available in the working world. Many must endure positions for security reasons. But in the volunteer community, we can say "no" to a position that will not bring us satisfaction. It is better for everyone that we do say "no" to opportunities that won't inspire enthusiasm. They are better done by someone else.

SELF-ASSESSMENT

"A man has to live with himself, and he should see to it that he always has good company."
—C. E. Hughes

How often have your heard, "Today is the beginning of the rest of your life?" It's true. Start now! But start with a plan, one built *after* you have had a good look at yourself.

What do you want out of life? What challenges do you thrive on? What mountains do you want to climb? What skills and talents do you possess that will help assure success?

To help you to focus on your strengths, try selecting words from the following choices that seem to describe you the best.

1	2	3	4
forceful	enthusiastic	systematic	patient
adventurous	outgoing	diplomatic	loyal
demanding	emotional	conscientious	stable
daring	sociable	conventional	team-oriented
decisive	generous	analytical	calm
self-assured	convincing	sensitive	deliberate
competitive	trusting	accurate	passive

If most of your choices are from column 1, you are probably good at initiating new ideas, getting results, making decisions, solving problems and taking authority.

The terms listed in column 2 reflect individuals who tend to be good at stimulating (motivating), entertaining, generating enthusiasm, interacting with others and offering assistance.

If, on the other hand, you selected more words from the third column, you are apt to be better at following directions, working with specific assignments, being diplomatic and doing critical thinking.

Those in the last column describe individuals who generally demonstrate patience and understanding, are loyal, act as good listeners, can work a with few new challenges and are good at concentrating.

This information can be used as a springboard. Start a page and begin to describe yourself, as you see yourself. Then, using the same lists, consider whether you could also identify areas that are difficult for you. For example, those who select more descriptive words from the first column may find they are not very cautious, or good at calculating risks. They may be uncomfortable in a protected environment, or researching and deliberating.

Those of you who chose more words from column 2 may have trouble working alone, or just with ideas. You may have difficulty concentrating, or seeking out facts and considering new ideas. These are just considerations, intended to get you focusing on how you function.

The serene, complacent volunteer of the third column, may have difficulty with critical thinking, acting independently, delegating or making decisions, especially unpopular ones.

Patient loyal workers described in column 4 may have trouble with change, or working under pressure, with too many expectations, or where considerable physical energy is needed.

With this in mind, you may want to look for positions which 1. have considerable freedom, with prestige and challenge, or 2. have many social activities, with little need for detail work and allow you to share ideas, or 3. assure security and a sense of being a part of the group in a comfortable, familiar setting, or 4. provide traditional procedures in a designated area of activity, where appreciation is shown.

People all have qualities and needs represented in each area listed—but tend to be more like one set of descriptive words than another.

VOLUNTEER OPPORTUNITIES

Once you have begun to clarify for yourself just what sort of a worker you are, consider the requirements of the challenge being offered to you. This may change annually as you are asked to wear still another hat from one year to the next. Each job offers different challenges, and you may be equipped to deal with some better than with others. Each past experience builds new skills.

New Challenges

Consider your newest volunteer opportunity. Must you:

✤ Initiate new program or ideas?

✤ Be prepared to make unpopular decisions?

✤ Display diplomacy?

✤ Deal with complete strangers, perhaps in a coalition?

❖ Do future planning?

❖ Deal exclusively with detail work?

❖ Take calculated risks?

❖ Organize the efforts of others?

❖ Endure basically boring work, filled with repetition?

❖ Be responsible for stimulating (motivating) others?

❖ Follow to the letter plans developed by someone else?

❖ Delegate to others.

❖ Provide skill training to new members?

❖ Deal with people problems?

❖ Be responsible for public speaking?

❖ Endure perpetual change and constant interruption?

❖ Be responsible for developing policy?

❖ Patiently follow specific instructions?

❖ Integrate new programs into an existing system?

Just what is being asked of you? Do you have a job description and a clear idea of what is expected of you? This should be provided by those who suggested you take on the new task.

Beyond all this, what do you really want from your involvement in a volunteer organization? Why do you belong? Make a list. Now rank these reasons. Look at your list again. This time rank each item in terms of the availability of opportunity to meet each need through this organization and this particular challenge.

Fish Exercises   Another exercise you might try—to come to know yourself better—is to pretend you are fishing and that the potential catch includes:

wisdom	happiness	faith	popularity
health	fame	honesty	courage
love	power	friends	skill
creativity	excitement	beauty	wealth

You have had a good day and you have caught the five fish you had hoped to catch. Check these (they should be those things you value most). However, while you doze off on the bank of the river, two get away. Mark out these two from your catch. Then, along comes your best friend, and he's hungry. You give him one of your fish (cross it off). And, while you talk, a cat sneaks up and runs off with another fish—leaving you with just one. Which is it? It is probably what you value most . . . what are you doing to see to it that your time is spent in activities that will provide you with this?

The world needs differences. We balance one another. Some people are simply better equipped to handle (and derive satisfaction from) different challenges. The trick is to determine in advance what you need and thrive on. Don't say "yes" just to please. To really get the most out of your volunteer experience, you have needs that must be satisfied.

To have a really successful committee or project, someone is needed who will generate new ideas, a marketing person to promote them, dependable workers to follow through, and a detail person to keep the group on track and within necessary guidelines. You probably could fill one of these slots better than another.

QUESTIONS FOR SELF-ANALYSIS

The following questions have been designed to get you thinking—to take time out to focus on why you are doing what you are doing—and in some cases to consider how you might improve your situation.

✤ Why am I volunteering?

✤ What are my strengths as a volunteer?

✤ What are my weaknesses as a volunteer?

✤ How can I measure my effectiveness as a volunteer?

✤ To what degree are my volunteer activities planned?

✤ Do I allow for individual differences among co-workers in my volunteer activities?

✤ What are my objectives for each volunteer activity?

✤ How can I measure the accomplishment of my volunteer activities?

✤ Am I good at:
  ✓ Lecturing
  ✓ Demonstrating
  ✓ Facilitating activities?

✤ What is my favorite activity? Why?

✤ Do I show flexibility as a volunteer?

✤ What skills are most important in my volunteer activities?

✤ Are there any skills I would like to acquire? How could I gain this skill or knowledge?

✤ What sort of volunteer do I enjoy working with most?

✤ What response or involvement do I expect from volunteer efforts?

✤ In what way does my volunteer effort make a difference to others?

The answers will only be as good as the use to which you will put them. The responses should help you to focus realistically on areas that are most apt to assure satisfaction. Each volunteer opportunity should meet not only the needs of the agency or group but *your* needs.

You might also ask yourself whether the volunteer challenge you most enjoyed:

✦ Called upon skill or knowledge

✦ Allowed you control over how and what you did

✦ Put you in a position of authority

✦ Gave you a chance to help others

✦ Increased your feeling of self-worth

✦ Provided an adventure or challenge

✦ Was cause for recognition from others

✦ Gave you a chance to learn and grow

Knowing what factors are important to you can help you to select volunteer opportunities that are most apt to meet your needs. A good match of volunteer challenge and your needs is important to you *and* the agency.

ASSESSING OURSELVES AS LEADERS

Once you accept a leadership position and have thought about the kind of leader you would like to become, make an assessment of your present capabilities. This chart can help you as well as the following self-disclosure exercises. These are useful to you only to the extent that you learn more about yourself and make use of the information revealed.

© 1994 Emily Kittle Morrison, *Leadership Skills*, Fisher Books, Tucson, Arizona

LEADERSHIP ASSESSMENT

IN MY LEADERSHIP ROLES I SEE MYSELF AS ABLE TO:	MOST OF THE TIME	SOME OF THE TIME	NEED TO IMPROVE
1. Sense the attitudes and feelings of myself and others			
2. Develop leadership in other members of a group			
3. Delegate responsibility to appropriate people			
4. Tolerate differences of views and opinion			
5. Find creative solutions to problems and conflicts			
6. Establish work assignments and spell out expectations			
7. Face mistakes, accept responsibility, and move on			
8. Be flexible			
9. Identify and analyze group problems			
10. Bring out the best efforts in others and show appreciation			
11. Seek help from others in a group			
12. Evaluate myself and others constructively and fairly			

How could you capitalize on your strengths?
What could you do to improve in your areas of weakness?

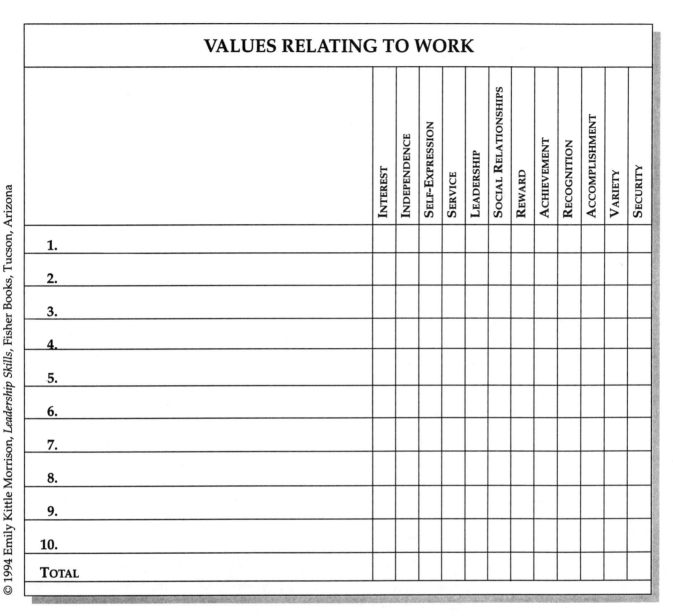

© 1994 Emily Kittle Morrison, *Leadership Skills*, Fisher Books, Tucson, Arizona

In the 10 spaces, list paid or unpaid work, programs, projects or activities that you have done because they were important to you.

Check each of the columns that seem appropriate for each of the positions you have listed on the form (definitions on following page). Total the responses in each column on the value sheet.

This is designed to help you determine the strength of your values as related to your work or volunteer activities. Suggested next step:

On a fresh sheet of paper, write a paragraph or two on each of the following:

What I have learned about myself and my work values?

The work value that appears the most and least.

VALUES RELATING TO WORK*

Interest   Any activity you did because you really liked doing it. This is one of your special interests and you find it stimulating.

Independence   An activity you liked because you could work alone, without a lot of supervision and direction from others. You like the feeling of being independent.

Self-Expression   Any activity that allowed you to use your natural talent or ability, where you could express who you really are and what you do well.

Service   Anything you did because it had meaning for others or because it was for another person's benefit. You have a need to help others and like to do a good and useful job wherever you are needed.

Leadership   Activities you did because you liked challenging your leadership abilities. You enjoyed planning and organizing and got a feeling of satisfaction from knowing that you could direct the activities of others.

Social Relationships   Any activity that you enjoyed because of the pleasure you get from doing things with others.

Reward   Activities you did because you knew you would receive a reward of some kind, such as money, approval or a special privilege.

Achievement   An activity you did because growth and development are important to you. You like to do things well and to do your best when you can do measurable assignments.

Recognition   Any activity you did because recognition of your work by others is important to you. You like being respected, having prestige and receiving approval for what you do.

Accomplishment   An activity that is accomplished because of your involvement, such as a program presented or project put into action. You are particularly task-oriented and like measurable results.

Variety   An activity you did because you like to do new things. You don't like routine or repetitious work.

Security   Any activity you did because you felt comfortable doing it. You were familiar with this and you like to do the things you find easy to do.

*Based on material in *How To Decide—A Workbook For Women*, by Nellie Tumlin Scholz, Judith Sosebee Prince & Gordon Miller. Avon Books, © 1976.

DATA, PEOPLE AND THINGS

The following is one final activity you might try to determine a productive direction for your volunteer efforts.

Working with Data

Check one of the three choices listed below.

❑ 1. I prefer work that is uncomplicated and easy to learn. I don't mind using information in a simple way if it doesn't require too much mental energy.

❑ 2. I like keeping track of and working with information in an orderly way. I prefer having others responsible for directing this work.

❑ 3. I enjoy organizing and administering information, as well as planning and developing ideas and new ways of doing things.

Involvement with People

Check one of the three choices listed below

❑ 1. I prefer involvement with information or things, though I don't mind a minimal interaction with people.

❑ 2. I like organizing and inspiring other people to do things.

❑ 3. I enjoy entertaining people and being the key person in a group.

Dealing with Things

Check one of the three choices listed below

❑ 1. I prefer little involvement with things. If I must work with things, I prefer uncomplicated, easy-to-learn procedures.

❑ 2. I enjoy running equipment with care and efficiency, but I prefer that someone else have responsibility for directing the work.

❑ 3. I enjoy using my hands to work with intricate tools and machines, and I like to be responsible for complex equipment that I understand.

A check in box 1 indicates low interest in the area of Data, People or Things. A check in box 2 refers to a moderate interest and a check in box 3 a high or considerable interest in the category.

Once you have determined whether your highest interest lies with Data, People or Things you are in a better position to select volunteer opportunities that will satisfy you and meet the needs of your organization. The success ratio is greatly improved if volunteers commit themselves to activities that meet their inner needs.

After you have considered the options listed above, you might find that you have a high interest in more than one area. This is lucky for you and your organization. It implies that you bring considerable enthusiasm in a variety of areas. To select the best avenue for you at this time consider the ramifications of each specific opportunity offered. Does it fit your time schedule? Is it in a location that suits you? Would you enjoy the co-workers? Is the environment one in which you would thrive? Is the 'cause' of great importance to you?

GROUP ASSESSMENT

The real reason for doing any sort of Group Assessment is to remedy problems and plot a successful course for the future.

The term "management by crisis" has been applied to business. Regrettably, the same is often true in many organizations. It comes from the failure to identify trends, assess interests, set realistic objectives and do reasonable future planning.

Future planning should focus on a failure to engage total quality management resources and build on strengths. When planning for the future of your organization, consider the following factors:

✤ The needs and goals of the general membership, not just your Board

✤ The needs of those you serve

✤ The priorities of the volunteers, as well as of the community

✤ The potential resources available to you from the community at large

✤ The implications of major areas of change, such as technology or the environment

✤ The manpower, within your group, available and interested in being actively involved

✤ The trends of the community at large, as well as the economy

It means remaining flexible, and viewing the task as *ongoing*.

Future planning requires a real commitment to the organization or agency and a sincere interest in ensuring the success of its programs and projects in a world where everything is changing. It means having a positive outlook and a belief in the ability of members and staff to prepare for this new world with its new challenges. It means caring about the people who will make it happen and dealing with the obstacles as well as the opportunities. It means involving everyone affected by the decisions in the decision-making process. It means remaining flexible and viewing the task as ongoing.

NEEDS ASSESSMENT

If the group is going to remain active and continue to be motivated, it is essential to periodically do some sort of "Needs Assessment." Members will not perform at their optimum level if their needs are not being met. With this in mind, before planning for the coming year, consider developing a questionnaire that will help assess the feelings of those you hope to involve and satisfy.

For example:

✤ Are they happy with the basic purpose of your group? If not, is it time to reconsider your reason for being?

✤ Do they like the format of your meetings, the frequency as well as the time and location? If not, what would be their preference?

❖ Is the structure of your organization workable, considering current challenges? If not, how might you reorganize to be more effective?

❖ Do your volunteers have the skills needed to perform the tasks expected of them? If not, would they be receptive to skill training and who could present this?

❖ Do they feel they, as volunteers, have a voice in the decisions being made? If not, what is their objection and how could the situation be improved?

❖ Is there adequate communication? If not, what changes could be made to assure that those in need of information have prompt, first-hand access to it?

❖ Are the lines of communication and authority clear and acceptable? If not, what changes would bring about greater satisfaction?

❖ What are the personal motives of your volunteers? Are your programs and activities planned with these in mind?

Do you ever wonder how your volunteers or members view your organization? Why is it that so few seem to do so much? To find the answer, consider developing a questionnaire to be filled out. To ensure that you get input from almost everyone (especially those who often are not there) mail the form with a stamped, self-addressed return envelope to those who were absent. Then, call individuals to encourage their response.

PART I The following two sets of questions will help you build a workable questionnaire.

1. Personal characteristics of your members:
   Age group _____
   Marital status _____
   Age of youngest child _____
   Years with the organization _____
   Employed? Full _____ Part time _____
   Board experience (with the organization)_____

2. What are they looking for with their involvement in your group? _____

3. What have they liked about their association?
   Most? _____
   Least? _____

4. How do they feel the community sees your organization?_____

5. Have they enjoyed the opportunities provided? _____

6. Do they tend to feel: Overworked? _____ Overlooked?_____

7. Have the meeting times or assignments been:
   Good for their schedule? _____
   In conflict?_____

8. Has the frequency of the involvement been reasonable? _____

9. Is the location convenient? _____

10. Do they feel a part of the decision-making? _____

PART 2   This section is designed to have volunteers consider the importance, to them, of 8 items regarding their feelings and involvement with your organization. In the portion designated A they are to list the importance of these factors and in B the degree of satisfaction they find through your current structure.

A				GROUP ASSESSMENT	B			
EXTREMLY IMPORTANT	IMPORTANT	OF SOME IMPORTANCE	NO DIFFERENCE		COMPLETELY SATISFIED	COULD BE BETTER	BARELY SATISFIED	UNSATISFIED
				Feeling needed by others				
				Working with interesting people				
				Chance to improve myself				
				Chance to serve in a key position				
				Being active in the community				
				Doing interesting things and getting away from routine				
				Developing friendships				
				Doing specific tasks that are of interest to me				

© 1994 Emily Kittle Morrison, *Leadership Skills*, Fisher Books, Tucson, Arizona

If the group numbers fewer than 50, many open-ended questions could be added. If larger, this would become time-consuming to tabulate.

It is usually good to remind the volunteers of the importance of being completely honest. And finally, before you ask that they take the time to share their views with you, be sure that you (in the position of leadership) are prepared to say in what manner you will use the information.

Are you willing to re-schedule your meeting times or assignments if these turn out to be areas of dissatisfaction? Would you arrange for social activities if there is great interest in these?

Could you develop a tool to determine areas of interest (such as a nominating questionnaire) if your volunteers feel overlooked? The individuals need to be assured that there is a real possibility for change.

With tools such as these there must be obvious follow-up. You must do something with the information: change a policy, change a program, find a better facility. Demonstrate that you read the information and are doing something about it. After this, the information should be used to re-establish your purpose, policies or program so that the needs of the participants are being met. Group members need to know they are being heard and appreciated.

GROUP ASSESSMENT ACTIVITIES
Clarify Expectations

Step 1: On a prepared form, have each member answer the following:

✓ List some of the things you hope this group will accomplish this year.
✓ List three things you hope your involvement will bring to you (what you hope to gain from volunteering).
✓ List what you feel the group should expect of its members.
✓ List special skills, leadership or services you feel you can contribute.

Step 2: Divide into pairs and let each individual interview a partner sharing their responses to the questions above.

Step 3: Separate the pairs and re-group to repeat step 2.

Step 4: Discuss the exercise with the group as a whole.

Step 5: Establish a list of expectations.

Step 6: Develop ideas for things to implement that will satisfy these expectations.

Unspoken Goals

On a large flip chart compile data from the entire group to determine how widely feelings are shared.

Step 1: Give each member 3 cards designated A, B and C.

Step 2: Ask each member to answer (anonymously) the following question on the appropriate card:

A. Why did you join this group?

B. What do you personally hope to gain from your membership?
C. What do you believe to be the goal of this group?

Step 3: Stack all of the cards by letter and divide into three groups. Each group is then asked to review the cards and compile a list of the ideas from their cards on newsprint (flip chart).

Step 4: Review the three lists with the group as a whole. Share feelings, acknowledge differences and recognize that personal needs will differ.

Step 5: This is a good starting point for zeroing in on agreement as to the real concerns of the group.

DEVELOP CLEAR GOALS

In advance of a meeting ask volunteers to complete the following statements:

I volunteered for this group because—
This group aims to—
I wish this group would—
I want our group to become—

At the meeting review the responses with the participants. Record the ideas on a flip chart in front of the group. Upon completion, discuss how well you are doing and what you could be doing to generally satisfy the members.

It is not necessary to try all of the above activities. However, if you are interested in assessing your group, consider making time for one of the exercises listed.

SKILL BANK

Having members fill out a questionnaire revealing their skills can be valuable when it comes time to pick officers and man projects and committees. It is also a way of assessing individual needs and areas of interest. It is an effective way to involve volunteers in activities, environments and time frames of their choosing.

Useful Information

The following represents information that could be useful.

❖ **Personal Data**
   Name, address, phone, schooling, spouse's name and occupation, dates of children's birth

❖ **Employment Status**
   Full or part time, employer, address, phone, position

❖ **Community Involvement**
   Organizations and positions (current and past)

❖ **Skills**
   Clerical (computer skills, typing, filing)

   Public contact (research, interviewing, public speaking, training, telephoning)

Media communication (writing copy, working with T.V., radio, paper)

Artist (design, layout, drawing)

Organizational (setting objectives, conducting meetings, supervising, planning, knowledge of bylaws or parliamentary procedure)

Ways and means (developing project ideas, writing proposals, preparing budgets; knowledge of community resources)

Research and education (research design, writing questionnaires, dealing with statistics)

Evaluating and reporting

Cultural arts (acting, crafts, photography, dancing, drama, music)

Special areas (i.e., working with children, elderly, handicapped, etc.)

Languages (country? sign? reading, speaking, writing)

✦ **Reasons for joining this group**

✦ **Positions held in this or other organizations**

✦ **In what capacity would you like to serve?**
(president, fund-raising chairman, docent, receptionist, etc.)

✦ **Volunteer involvement**
Types of activities, available time slots and kind of settings (i.e., in a group, working alone)

Should you choose to develop a Skill Bank, the material outlined above can be set in questionnaire form. Leave adequate space for people to fully respond to each section. Remember to use the information filed in a Skill Bank.

This information can be kept in a file box with various headings:

✦ Volunteers

✦ Skills

✦ Geographic area

✦ Times available

✦ Interests

✦ Other associations

Information can be placed in a Rolodex with similar divisions, or even more useful, entered into a computer database for access on a moment's notice.

GATHERING PRODUCTIVE DATA* When designing a questionnaire there are a number of different approaches you can use. Each technique produces a different kind of data The following outline reviews points for gathering productive data. See Appendix for how to design a questionnaire.

GATHERING PRODUCTIVE DATA			
TYPE OF RESPONSE	RESULTING DATA	ADVANTAGES	DISADVANTAGES
1. Fill-in-the-blank	Nominal	Less biasing, greater response flexibility	Harder to score, social bias affects response and interpretation
2. Scaled	Interval (Quantitative)	Easy to score	Time-consuming can be biasing
3. Ranking Procedure	Ordinal	Easy to score Forces respondent to make choice	Difficult to complete
4. Checklist	Nominal	Easy to score and to respond to	Fewer options provides less data

Examples

1. Looking at your present situation, what do you expect to be doing five years from now?

2. How do you feel about the proposed change in the membership requirements:

strongly approve	*approve*	*disapprove*	*strongly disapprove*

3. Please rank the following proposed fund-raisers in order of preference to you. (1 = most interesting, 6 = least interesting, (Rank only 4)

(Try to include all realistic options)

Black-tie Ball   _____
Cabaret   _____
Las Vegas night   _____
Art auction   _____
Rummage sale   _____
Christmas boutique   _____
Other (please specify)   _____

*Based on material in *Conducting Educational Research*, by Bruce Tuckman, Harcourt Brace Janovich, San Francisco CA, © 1972.

4. My current employment status is:

_____ (1) Work full time (paid employment)

_____ (2) Work part time (paid employment)

_____ (3) No paid employment

Notice *none* of the above features a "paragraph answer"—that kind of "soft information" is very hard to analyze on a large scale.

Pertinent questions to ask before designing a form: How would I enter the information into a computer database? How would I code it?

QUESTIONS FOR CONSIDERATION

The answers to these questions can be used to plan for the future. Each volunteer could be given a chance to respond.

❖ Are your needs being met? If so why: If not, why not?

❖ Do you feel comfortable with co-workers?

❖ Are you proud to be a part of this organization?

❖ How did you happen to join?

❖ How long do you expect to be involved?

❖ Are expectations for your efforts clear?

❖ Do you feel challenged? Do you feel appreciated?

❖ Do you have the resources you need to do the job?

❖ What do you tell others about your association with this group?

VOLUNTEER EXIT REVIEW

One way to determine the effectiveness of your volunteer program is to use a Volunteer Exit Review. Some volunteers will simply drop by the wayside, some will formally resign and others will leave a cloud of dust and dismay in their wake. To intercept factors that are agency-caused reasons for a person leaving, try using a Volunteer Exit Review. This is best done privately and anonymously.

A form such as the one shown on the following page can be sent with a self-addressed stamped envelope to the "dearly departed." Honesty is important. It must be pursued in a way that allows the former volunteer to tell you truthfully why he or she left.

The matter must not end here. The supervisor, director or Board president must be prepared to consider the responses objectively and to be willing to seek change for any factors that appear to the the cause of the dissatisfaction. After a few of these have been returned you will begin to get a picture of your program that profiles your strengths and weaknesses.

VOLUNTEER EXIT REVIEW

Dear Former Volunteer:

By way of evaluating and improving our program we are asking that you take a minute to answer the following questions.

1. What was your position with ABC agency?
   _____

2. How long had you been involved?
   _____

3. How would you describe your feelings about your association with ABC agency?
   _____

4. Do you feel you received adequate training and supervision?
   _____

5. Do you feel it was a rewarding experience?
   _____

6. Did you have a comfortable relationship with co-workers and/or staff? Comments:
   _____
   _____
   _____

7. Would you recommend to others that they become involved at ABC?
   _____

8. .Was your reason for leaving personal? _____
   Did you have a conflict with scheduling? _____
   Were you in some way dissatisfied with your experience? _____

   Can you describe this? _____

9. Could you offer any suggestions for the improvement of volunteer activities and relationships at ABC agency?

10. Have you any additional comments you would like to make?
    _____
    _____
    _____

Thank You For Your Help
Please return this form in the enclosed stamped envelope.

© 1994 Emily Kittle Morrison, *Leadership Skills*, Fisher Books, Tucson, Arizona

14

Publicity

"one good word begets another"

Most community service groups at one time or another want to share news about their activities, to solicit help or secure financial support for their projects.

There are certain guidelines the media expects you to follow when seeking free coverage. Although basically similar, these guidelines will vary somewhat from one station, magazine or paper to another.

Most local papers want material about interesting speakers or programs, charitable activities, awards presentations and elections. They will need to know if these are open to the public. Additionally, most papers want to print feature articles with a human-interest angle, such as three generations working to establish a worthy facility.

WHAT Providing information about your group or organization to the media puts your organization before the public in print, on television, or on radio. It lets others know what you are doing. It can allow your spokesperson's views to be quoted by a newspaper or in a television or radio broadcast.

Publicity can range from a brief mention in a round-up column, to a longer magazine feature; from a short announcement of a group activity on a radio broadcast, to an hour of air time.

HOW AND WHY   To generate news about your group or organization, have something newsworthy to share. Certain components make a story appealing. These are: timeliness, importance to community and human interest. The information has interest to the community.

Ċ The media, especially newspapers, need information that they cannot always gather themselves. They depend on organizations for story ideas and news about their own events. Newsworthy stories help the media and at the same time provide publicity for you.

Results   Publicity provides valuable exposure and recognition for your organization. Establishing a dialogue and creating contacts within the media that serve your geographical area ensures that they will have a better idea of what you are doing. Also, this helps to ensure that your side of the story is heard, even in negative situations.

NEWS RELEASES   A news (press) release is designed to let the media know of your planned project or event.

Several techniques are useful for generating publicity. Most basic is the news release—a story written in journalistic style and distributed to the appropriate media. Put the most important information: who, what, when, where, why and how—in the first paragraph. The following paragraphs provide more details of lesser importance.

In local newspapers, news releases are sometimes printed as is, or with minor editing. The lead paragraph may become the basis for a radio news story. News releases also provide background information to editors and news directors who assign reporters to develop a story.

Stories are also developed by local media from ideas suggested in letters, media alerts or telephone news tips. In all instances, it is essential that you provide information that the media consider newsworthy.

Story ideas have a better chance of receiving attention if they are directed to the *specific* editor, reporter or news director who covers your area of interest. Find out which reporter covers your area (education, health, youth issues) and what he or she looks for in a story. That very first person-to-person contact occasionally triggers a chain of events that leads to great publicity.

When to Use   Timing your publicity depends on the timeliness of your story. A quick-breaking news development can be relayed immediately by telephone or FAX. Notify the media at least two weeks in advance of your planned event.

Talk-show guests are usually booked eight weeks ahead, but slots may open up on short notice. Guests have to cancel sometimes. If your spokesperson can be available on short notice, you may be able to take advantage of a cancellation.

Points to Remember

- ❖ The media depend on information.
- ❖ Your story should be newsworthy.
- ❖ The most important elements should be in the first paragraph of a news release.
- ❖ The media need ample notice of forthcoming events.

Basic Guidelines for News Releases

Consider this checklist when preparing a release:

- ❖ Use the organization's letterhead or a special News Release form that identifies the organization, its purpose and adress. Include your name, address and phone as a contact person.
- ❖ Be newsworthy (timely, of importance, with prominent persons, in a special place, bringing about change, out of the ordinary, etc.).
- ❖ Submit notices only if the event is open to the public.
- ❖ Send to news editors two weeks in advance for daily and weekly publications . . . if possible.
- ❖ Prepare material with your audience in mind. Approach resources most likely to reach these people.
- ❖ Re-read your work with your reader in mind. Edit to ensure clarity and remove awkwardness.
- ❖ Copy should be brief and concise, accurate and timely.
- ❖ When providing background material state: *Who, What, Where, When, Why,* and *How.*
- ❖ Use first and last names. Include identification of persons named, such as office held (include office phone number only).
- ❖ Include all vital information.
- ❖ Indicate your preferred release date.
- ❖ Include a headline, presenting a summary of the story.
- ❖ Type or print your material on one side of 8-1/2 x 11 paper.
- ❖ Always double-space. Indent five spaces to begin a paragraph.
- ❖ Use 1-inch margins on all sides.
- ❖ Do not split a paragraph from one page to another.
- ❖ If more than one page is submitted, put "(more)" at the bottom of each page except the last page.
- ❖ At the end, type "-30-", three lines below the end of your copy.
- ❖ Page numbers and identification should appear on each sheet.
- ❖ Send good-quality copies to each publication and maintain at least one for your files.
- ❖ Proofread your work for accuracy of information, grammar and spelling. Then have someone else proofread it, too.

SAMPLE NEWS RELEASE

Contact name

Mailing address

City, state, zip code

(area code) phone number   (area code) FAX number

Identification Line (slug line)   **Release Date**
(such as *XYZ Organization National Convention*)

HEADLINE (all caps)

Copy (double-spaced, five spaces indent for paragraphs)

-30-

FACT SHEETS

A fact sheet presents information about your event in outline form. Use the same basic format as a News Release. In this case complete sentences are not needed, and it is not necessary to use paragraph form.

❖ List five *W's* and *How* (or more specific words) in caps at the left followed by a short answer

❖ Double space between elements

❖ Delete "more" and simply number additional sheets, if needed

SAMPLE FACT SHEET

Contact name

Mailing address

City, state, zip code

(area code) phone number   (area code) FAX number

Fact Sheet On (subject)   **Release Date**

What: _____

For Whom: _____

When:_____

Where: _____

Why:_____

How:_____

Cost: _____

Registration: _____

Speakers:_____

Programs: _____

Sponsors:_____

-30-

TIP SHEETS A "tip sheet" is used when inviting anyone from the media to come and cover your event. The form should briefly present *Who, What, Where, When,* and *Why. When* should be followed by the specific time and *Where* should include directions, if helpful.

PRESS KITS A press kit is a collection of material distributed before a press conference or with an especially newsworthy news release. It is usually contained in a folder and includes:

+ Cover letter

+ Your news release

+ A fact sheet

+ Photo(s)

+ Artist's renderings, if appropriate

+ Background material on your organization

+ Related material from an in-house newsletter

+ Your annual report, if appropriate

Photo Information Only certain types of photos are generally accepted by the media.

+ Most acceptable: photos taken by a professional photographer

+ Non-professional photos: a good-quality point-and-shoot auto-focus camera or a 35mm single-lens reflex will produce good photos

+ 8 X 10 black and white photos on glossy paper are preferred, but 4 X 5s are commonly used. Color prints may be acceptable but check first with the media to see if they can use them.

+ Polaroids are not acceptable.

+ Try to create an innovative setting without a distracting background

+ Select subject matter relating to your story

+ Try for a new angle; be original

+ Crop to eliminate extraneous background material

+ Provide good contrast of light and dark (but not too dark)

+ Photos must be in perfect condition

+ Include a brief and factual caption. It should state the pertinent slug line and contact data on the reverse side of the photo. **Do not write on the back of the photo.** Type information on a label or a sheet of paper and apply to the bottom back of photo with tape. **Never use paper clips on photographs.** The caption should be readable as you look at the photograph

NEWS COVERAGE   Broadcasters are under no obligation to grant time to any group. No law requires a station to devote a specific amount of time to community organizations. Even so, it has become a tradition among broadcasters to be sensitive to community needs and to communicate in the public interest.

Public Service Announcements   PSA announcements are only available to non-profit organizations (no time is available to promote bingo or lotteries). Many just like you are seeking free air time that is limited.

You must work in cooperation with the station and not expect any format changes or special arrangements. A taped or recorded announcement has the advantage of being available at numerous times, even if it is not as appealing as a live interview, or as long.*

Once you have made arrangements to meet with the Program Director, *be on time*, and arrive prepared. Written material for broadcasting falls into the same basic guidelines as that for print media. However, if a script is needed, be as informal as you would in a normal speaking situation. For an interview, provide a biographical sketch of the person to be interviewed, as well as six or eight points you hope to cover. Give phonetic spelling for difficult names.

Special programs are sometimes devoted to presentations, as are segments of regular programs. Also, there are:

Spots   Brief announcements made as time allows during the broadcast day

Personality Spots   Announcements made by recognizable personalities on behalf of a community project

News Items   Short stories included in a regular newscast, briefly discussing a newsworthy event

Editorials   Statements prepared that represent the station management's view on community programs or projects

Always telephone a station's Program Director for specific information regarding their public-service policy. Be familiar, in advance, with their programs so you know what you are talking about when you call.

Arrive prepared for any meeting with a Program Director. Know: *What* the basic message is that you want to relay; *Who* you want to reach (your audience), *How* to present your message in the best way.

*Many stations will help you to develop a useful video to use as a PSA.

TIME ALLOTMENTS

	RADIO TIME	TV TIME
10 seconds	25 words	20 words
20 seconds	50 words	40 words
30 seconds	75 words	60 words
60 seconds	150 words	125 words

For radio, use descriptive words so the listener can create a mental picture. For TV, provide at least one slide or photograph for each ten seconds (and here, matte-finish—not glossy—color photos are preferred). Request a return of your materials or they will be discarded (provide a self-addressed mailer for this purpose). Most stations now use video, even from a home-video camera.

For radio, remember that peripheral sounds are very distracting, (things such as papers shuffling, background conversations). In TV, softer colors are preferable to sharp contrast; showy accessories and fabrics with small prints or stripes do not transmit well and should be avoided.

After any presentation or article has appeared, a note of appreciation should be sent.

Use the following form to outline local media contacts. Never trust a media directory to be 100% accurate—they seldom are!

LOCAL MEDIA DATA				
	NAME Newspapers, Magazines or Stations	CONTACT Editors, Columnists and Broadcasters	ADDRESS or FAX	PHONE
NEWSPAPERS				
MAGAZINES				
RADIO STATIONS				
TELEVISION STATIONS				

GET ACQUAINTED

To open the channels of communication, consider having a speaker from your local TV or radio station speak at one of your meetings. This allows for great public relations. Your members will learn more about what the broadcasters do. The broadcasters will gain firsthand knowledge of your group.

PRINT MATERIAL

There are many categories of printed materials. Some are described in the following pages. Some require the services of a commercial printer. Although guidelines are described in this section, it is essential that you contact the printer you expect to use before you actually begin to prepare camera-ready copy. This meeting helps to ensure against the costly mistake of preparing material in the wrong size or in the wrong manner for the printer's equipment.

PRINTING

The term *printer* generally refers to a small- or medium-size commercial printing facility. Small-scale affordable printing service is available at *copy centers*. These are located in most areas and offer a variety of printing services with rapid turnover, expertise and quality to satisfy a variety of requirements.

Ideally, when you are ready to take your camera-ready copy to the printer, you should be fully prepared, having made all decisions regarding size, color, paper and quantity. Don't expect the printer to make these decisions. Make these decisons yourself, perhaps with guidance from the printer. The material must be thoroughly proofread; it is not the printer's responsibility to catch *your* errors.

Prepare your material well in advance of your actual deadline, to allow for the printer's schedule. Consider contracting with the printer to save a certain day each month for such things as newsletters. If you do this you must be responsible for your part of the commitment. If you plan to mail your materials, allow sufficient time to avoid unanticipated delays due to weather conditions, weekends or holidays. Stay in touch with your printer if you are producing something with a regular or time-sensitive print date.

POSTERS

Posters can be an effective, inexpensive way to convey your message. They can be mass-produced by silk-screen printing, or can be made individually. In each case always create a rough draft to develop your concept. Then sketch it onto your board in pencil.

For individual posters consider using wide felt markers or press type. Use letters large enough to be read easily from a distance. Graphics (art work of any kind) will greatly add to the eye appeal of your posters, as will key words like **Attention: Sale! Notice!**

Work neatly and with care. Keep the lines straight and uniform. Bright colors have general appeal, but avoid gaudy shades and orange (hard to read from a distance). All pertinent information should appear and be easy to read. It should be laid out in an eye-catching and memorable way.

Create a full-size sample and check it carefully. Place it at the distance it will probably be viewed and check whether you can read it. You may have to make it larger, use larger type, or simplify the message.

Your next concern is for your audience. Where could you place the posters to reach those of most interest to you? schools? churches? shops? supermarkets? gas stations? Be sure to obtain permission from the management before displaying any advertising material.

FLYERS   Flyers require the same considerations as posters, except they are smaller and printed in bulk. Brevity, neatness and creativity will increase your chances of having it read.

The printing part implies that you must keep in mind the guidelines of camera-ready copy.

The method of reproduction you choose for your flyer will depend on your budget and how important it is that your material look professional. Copiers can produce adequate results for most needs.

Photocopies (such as Xerox™) can be quite expensive in the long run if you don't have access to a machine. Depending on quantity, offset copies can be run more reasonably and give greater clarity.

NOTE: To test the ultimate effect of your draft, and to see if it has all been laid out correctly, make one photocopy before ordering offset copies.

DIRECT MAIL   Direct mail is the most expensive advertising approach because mailing costs are added to the printing costs. Direct mail reaches your audience directly and allows the reader time to consider your information.

Use direct mail *only* when you are certain of your audience and have access to an *accurate* mailing list. Figure that most mailing lists change 20% per year. It costs real money to mail to someone who has moved away. The post office only forwards first-class mail for a short time. They do not forward bulk mail.

If you are sending a letter, give it a personal touch. Send along an informative fact sheet. Appearance is of the greatest importance. Type or print your letter on white paper with a carbon ribbon or use a computer. Place the material carefully on the page. Each copy should look like an original. Where possible use a word processor with an ink-jet or a laser printer.

NEWSLETTERS   The first thing you will be involved with is the layout of your copy. Copy can be prepared using a computer word-processing or publishing program or a good typewriter. If you plan to type your material, it is important to know that reproductions made from a carbon-ribbon typewriter (or a laser or ink-jet printer if you have access to a computer) provide better quality than a typewriter with a cloth ribbon. Typing with a carbon ribbon produces clean, dark letters. Type on regular bond paper and correct with correction tape.

LAYOUT TECHNIQUE   If you are taking your material to a printer to layout, you will be charged for this service. Create a *dummy* showing what the final product will look like in the form of pages.

Begin by determining how much material you have and how much space it will take. After this you can create a *dummy* of paper folded to represent your final booklet or newsletter. For example, one sheet folded becomes 4 pages: front, left middle, right middle and back. Each time you add a page, you really add 4. When you fold a second sheet, you create an 8-page *dummy.*

Having determined how much space your material will need, then decide how you want to lay it out. You will discover that your paper will be numbered out of order for printing. As an example, if you are planning an 8-page booklet, your sheets will look like those at the bottom of this page.

An article beginning on page 5 and continuing on page 6 will be laid out on separate sheets of your camera-ready copy.

If you would like to use fewer final sheets of paper (because printers charge by the sheet), consider laying out your material on paper 10-2/3 x 13-3/4 and reduce the material by 25% to be printed on 8-1/2 x 11. Or, you could prepare it on 17 x 22 to be reduced 50%, to be printed on 8-1/2 x 11. But this usually makes the print *too small.* Keep in mind the visual capabilities of your readers. Older readers prefer large type that is easy to read, such as 12-point type. Always do a test sample before printing an entire edition or issue.

There may be a small charge for reduction, but a considerable savings in paper cost. Run the maximum number of copies that can be used at one time—prices go down by volume. Avoid making the common mistake of running too many copies. There are basic charges which will be repeated each time you reprint. Two-sided printing is only 90% more expensive than a one-sided sheet. Two one-sided sheets cost more.

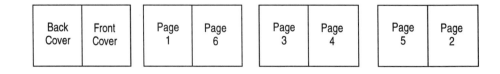

When doing your own final layout, you can create bold headlines by using press type (rub-on letters) or clip art, available at stationery, college bookstores, and art-supply stores. These letters can be pressed onto graph paper (with pale-blue lines) to spell out the needed headings.

To add eye appeal to your newsletter, black-and-white line drawings and borders may be reproduced from clip-art books. Avoid clutter. For ideas about effective placement, look at magazines. Leave enough *white space* to create a balanced effect and a half inch of *grip edge* for the machine to grip your material at the top, or bottom during printing. Your printer can tell you more about this.

Computer Programs   Most personal computers with a word-processing program and a laser or ink-jet printer are capable of producing the clean, sharp copy that you can supply as camera-ready copy to the printer. Check out the word-processing programs adaptable for home and office computers. Some software companies offer software that contains a variety of letter, brochure and newsletter formats that you can adapt to your own needs. It is likely that someone on your staff or Board will be able to help. If not, try to specifically recruit a volunteer for such a challenge.

In many cases, you will find it cost-effective to use someone who offers this service for a fee. Such persons are often referred to as specialists in *DesktopPublishing*.

COPY PREPARATION
Practical Points in Making Camera-Ready Copy

❖ Type your copy on white bond paper using an electric typewriter with a carbon ribbon or use a computer with a word-processing or publishing program and a laser or ink-jet printout.

❖ Make typing corrections with correction tape; do not use onion paper or textured paper. Do not erase.

❖ Notes to the printer may be made in the margin using light-blue pencil that does not reproduce.

❖ Captions, borders, pictures and such should be secured with rubber cement; this allows for changes.

❖ Cartoons, borders and captions can be reproduced from sources such as such as clip-art books which provide permission for their materials to be reproduced. Reproduction of printed materials from books, magazines or newspapers without securing permission violates copyright laws.

❖ Art-supply stores and college bookstores sell transfer (or press-type) letters for use in captions and headlines. These products can help reduce the cost of typesetting but should not be used for large amounts of copy because of the expense and time required to apply.

❖ Enlargements and reductions of drawings, tables and graphs will add to your cost, but you can reduce the number of camera settings at the printer by enlarging or reducing line drawings and large type on a high-quality copier capable of the process. Use these copies in pasting up your camera-ready copy.

❖ Photographs submitted to a printer can be in black and white or color. Color photo prints cost less than black-and-white prints, typically, because more color-processing equipment is available.

❖ Color reproduction on a printing press requires four colors to be printed. It is terribly expensive, so you probably won't often choose that method of reproducing your materials.

❖ Red reproduces as black; most other colors as shades of gray. If you are in doubt, a good rule-of-thumb method to help predict what the printed results will be is to make a photocopy of a sample of your prepared material. The printed results may be very similar.

❖ In the end, you (*not* the printer) are ultimately responsible for any errors made in the camera-ready preparation! Proofread before and after the copy is set in type. Get someone else to proofread the copy, too. One proofreader is *not* sufficient. You can never proofread enough—errors are often obvious *after* they are printed.

❖ Plan ahead to avoid delays and to save on costs.

- Costs can be reduced it you are able to use several photographs at the same percentage of reduction or enlargement because the camera operator may be able to photograph several of them together. Or, he may be able to use the same camera setting for more than one photo or illustration.

- Check with your printer to learn how any covers will be printed and whether you can afford to print with more than one color of ink. The printer will provide a cost estimate that will help you to make a affordable choices regarding paper stock and the number of ink colors to be used.

- Prepare your original in black and white, unless you'll use a color copier for multicolor duplication. If the job is to be printed in more than one color, check with the printer to see how he would like the camera-ready copy prepared. You can also use black ink on color paper or textured stock for anything other than news releases.

- Camera-ready copy (with the exception of photographs that will be processed separately) should be prepared in a consistent size to allow the camera operator to make camera shots (to produce offset-printing negatives) at *one* camera setting (reduction or enlargement). Exceptions which require individual camera settings will add to the time and cost.

- Check camera-ready copy by viewing it on a light table (or by checking it against the lines of graph paper). Inaccurately prepared copy will result in additional costs and delays.

- Printers have equipment that staple, collate, saddle-stitch (sewing or stapling in the center fold), drill holes and fold (in various configurations, depending on the number of pages).

- Depending on the printing method, printing on two sides may require additional time to allow the first side to dry before the second side is printed. Collating, folding, drilling and stapling also require time.

- Request a schedule from your printer as early in your planning as possible.

15

Career
Development

"From the House to the Senate"

This chapter is about doing anything you set your mind to do. It takes planning. It will take an investment of time and effort but great steps can be taken through volunteer placement—*quality* volunteer placement. The first step is to get to know yourself—what you value, what you enjoy and what you do well.

Have you developed marketable skills such as advertising or selling ads for your news magazine or program? Or done graphic work, such as layouts for either of the above? Perhaps you have been a conference coordinator or tour guide. Have you administered a large project or initiated a new program? These concrete experiences can be used in moving from volunteer to paid staff.

MAKE IT HAPPEN Begin to look at what you have done in terms of achievements and gaining specific knowledge. Open your thinking. Consider where, in the world of employment, there might be a market for these skills. Then develop a marketing plan to sell yourself to a specific employer in a specific position.

Don't rely on an employment agency to find something for you, and don't expect to discover that "great find" in the classified ads. You will probably have to make it happen yourself. *You* need to take charge. It is *your* life. It should be *your* choice.

It is possible to parlay your skills, experience and understanding from a volunteer activity into a staff position with the same organization. Submit an application when an opening develops. Chances are you already have a known track record and associates to speak on your behalf. Available positions often go to people who are already known by the organization.

Most dependable people, having leadership experience from the volunteer community, possess the skills needed to do many non-technical administrative jobs and to supervise others.

Most social-service organizations have some paid staff. At any one time, an organization may be looking for a person with the very kind of skills volunteer leaders have acquired. Look in the Yellow Pages, visit your local Volunteer Bureau or Voluntary Action Center. Of the agencies listed, which sound most interesting to you? Research them fully. Then develop a sales pitch designed to sell yourself to the organization of your choice. Convince them that they can't live without you!

You may not have a college degree or professional background, but you may have the "Equivalent Experience." This is true not only in specific social-service agencies but with groups such as professional fund-raisers.

Once you secure just one paid position you put yourself into a different category when it comes to looking for work. You have a recent successful experience doing something you can document.

For women just entering the paid work force, Shirley Fader recommends in *From Kitchen to Career*, that you look at your pre-marriage occupation and add your volunteer work to the picture. What you have is a new mix of talent, training and experience that can be parlayed into a lucrative position, if you are willing to make it happen.

This requires a bit of creative thinking, such as the ideas suggested above. You may have insight that no one else possesses and can create a job that did not exist before. Recognize that you *do* have valuable expertise to market! Convince potential employers that they need you. Be specific about what you can do for them and document your experience. (See Functional Resumé Guidelines at end of this chapter).

Consider writing a grant with yourself as the key player. Once you are aware of specific community needs you are in a position to design and develop a position. Most agency directors would welcome your help and be receptive to your interest—especially if you have a way of funding the proposed position.

An important step toward a paid position (utilizing volunteer experience) is to begin to *network*. The people you meet in professional associations are probably the first ones to know about openings. Philanthropic groups such as The Association of Volunteer Administrators, the American Society for Training and Development, Junior Leagues, Rotary Clubs and other such associations provide not only great training but contacts as well.

THE IDEAL JOB   What would your ideal job look like? Can you describe it? What kind of activity interests you?

+ How many hours a week do you want to work?

+ In what kind of setting?

+ Would you prefer working with tasks or people?

+ Do you want to work on your own?

+ Do you want structure and guidance or freedom to be creative and responsible for your own time?

+ What sort of people would you find interesting as co-workers, as supervisors, as recipients of your service?

+ What skills and talents do you want to use?

+ What kinds of things do you have experience doing and what do you like to work with—cameras, food, computers, phones, numbers, paper, etc.?

TARGET MARKETING YOURSELF   If you have the luxury, consider entering the field of your choice by offering to work on a specific project (administrating, fund raising, ad selling) to prove yourself. Up to this point you have been working on a voluntary basis anyway! You might request a fee to be calculated as a percentage of ads solicited or funds raised.

Whether you are looking for your first real job, returning to work after years away, finding a position after being laid off or simply looking for a change—securing a position ultimately depends on how prepared you are. You will need to explore specific openings and establish why you are the best person to consider. How articulate you are, how much self-assurance you radiate and how positive you appear will determine your ultimate success. You may find your position over lunch or while working side by side with someone on a disaster-relief effort, or after serving on a Board. Not all positions are filled after a formal interview.

+ Figure out what you do best and where you could do it (see Chapter 13, *Self-Assessment*).

+ Present yourself to an employer of your choice (even if he or she does not yet realize the need for you).

+ Go to your job search with a well-constructed resumé (an advertisement that promotes *you*).

+ Develop a complete marketing plan in which you are the featured product.

SAMPLING OF DOCUMENTATION

- ✤ Functional Resumé
- ✤ Job descriptions
- ✤ Letters of commendation
- ✤ Citations/awards/certificates
- ✤ News clippings
- ✤ Samples of your work:
  Displays, exhibits, posters, press release, flyers, brochures, workshops, written proposals, photographs, slide shows, developed manuals, charts, graphs, maps, articles you have written.
- ✤ Audio or visual tapes:
  Tapes depicting you in action—speaking, training, counseling, interviewing or demonstrating
- ✤ Letters of recommendation:
  Letters written by agency executives, local leaders, city planners.

Volunteer opportunities provide on-the job training, a chance at an internship as well as an opportunity to determine (at little risk) whether a position in a particular field would be satisfying. Teenagers who face the obstacle of *Experience Required* can profit from volunteer involvement. Time invested in a volunteer position not only provides documented experience but many times it opens doors by providing contacts for paid positions.

To realistically plan for a career, and to use your volunteer activity as a springboard, review Chapter 13, *Self-Assessment*. Without a clear picture of who you are and what you can do, it is difficult to develop a reasonable plan about where you might go and how you could get there.

Focus on your *achievements* (activities that gave you a feeling of pride), rather than merely your *accomplishments* (which are things you simply did). Concentrating on these activities will help you to get a good idea of what would be satisfying in the working world.

CREDIT FOR VOLUNTEER SKILLS

Continuing Education Units (C.E.U.) represent ten contact hours of participation in an organized, continuing education experience under responsible sponsorship, capable direction and qualified instruction. These C.E.U.s carry no academic credit, nor are they accompanied by grades. The type of training they catalog is considered "post secondary." Many community colleges award C.E.U.s for their non-credit courses. These units quantify and validate training.

Remember to keep track of any such training that offers *certification* or C.E.Us.

If you are transferring volunteer experience to a U.S. Civil Service job, you will find C.E.U.s recognized in determining entry to mid-level technical and professional jobs.

THE RESUMÉ Each year, perhaps as an easy reminder on your birthday, revise your resumé. Add all of your latest accomplishments, achievements, awards and recognitions. Itemize programs planned and changes initiated, document your successes and your skills gained.

Your resumé should be created with consideration for the position you seek. This tool is all some potential employers will use in deciding whether to offer you an interview. It should be honest and forthright and market you well. Keep in mind the following key points when developing your resumé.

DO

- Prepare a cover letter describing briefly what is enclosed and why it is of importance to the potential employer. Sign boldly and legibly.

- Organize your resumé in outline form where possible. Otherwise, use short, concise sentences.

- Use strong **action verbs** ("**Directed** $50,000 Fund-Raiser"—rather than "**was appointed** chairman of the Rummage Sale").

- List your achievements on an attached sheet in descending order of importance.

- Follow an itemized list with a functional list, to better convince the employer that your volunteer skills are transferable.

- Make laser or ink-jet copies or have your resumé professionally printed or copied so each page looks like a clear original.

DO NOT

- Use a service to write your resumé; you risk becoming too much like someone else's packaged product.

- Use gimmicks such as colorful paper, exaggerated typefaces, over-size paper, catchy borders. *Do* prepare a professional-looking form.

- Explain why you left your last job.

- Abuse your friendships by expecting too much from those you ask to serve as references. *Do* keep references to a minimum and of a professional nature. On your resumé you might use the phrase: "References upon request."

- State a salary requirement or mention a previous one.

- Adapt someone else's resumé. *Do* start at the beginning and create your own material using a resumé guide such as the one at the end of this chapter.

- Distort the truth or purposely mislead.

- Editorialize or write in the third person.

**FUNCTIONAL
RESUMÉ
GUIDELINES***
(Suggestions)

Name   Date
Address
City, State, Zip Code
Telephone   Fax

❖ **Objective**
(Position sought)

❖ **Education**
(Include degrees and honors)

❖ **Past Employment**

❖ **Skills and Experience**
(Use only if applicable)
✓ Administrative
(Organized, Coordinated, Implemented, Designed, Initiated, Supervised, Directed, Activated)
✓ Parliamentary Law/By-laws Interpretation
(Put together, Interpreted, Acted as, Translated, Appointed to)
✓ Public Speaking/Educator
(Compiled, Debated, Addressed, Spoke to, Moderated, Trained)
✓ Advocacy
(Evaluated, Advocated for, Presented, Provided)
✓ Financial Management/Budgeting
(Reviewed, Studied, Developed, Participated in, Assisted in, Executed)
✓ Leadership
(Elected, Acted as, Administered, Presided over, Proposed, Executed)
✓ Project Development
(Originated, Planned, Delegated, Participated in, Advocated for)
✓ Communication
(Wrote, Edited, Drafted, Summarized, Interpreted)
✓ Research
(Designed, Drafted, Reviewed, Researched, Developed)
✓ Training
(Workshop Experience in, Seminars attended, Conferences participated in, Conventions attended, Independent course work completed)

❖ **References:**
(Organization presidents, volunteer directors, agency directors, etc.)

❖ **Conclusion:**
Conclude with your perception of the qualifications needed for the position you are seeking and how well you feel your background has prepared you to succeed in such a position.

THE INTERVIEW

1. **Prepare for the interview:**
   - ✓ Practice your interview technique in the privacy of your own home or with a friend to experience a "dry run in a low-stress environment."
   - ✓ If possible schedule your appointment before lunch, early in the week.

2. **The command of the interview belongs with the *interviewer*. However:**
   - ✓ Arrive early, dressed professionally (avoid strong colognes and bold jewelry).
   - ✓ Consider carrying a good-looking briefcase (if it is appropriate to the position you are seeking).
   - ✓ Be cordial and pleasant.
   - ✓ Shake hands firmly and look directly into the eyes of the interviewer when you introduce yourself.
   - ✓ Sit close to the desk; sit tall and lean toward the interviewer (this implies interest and attentiveness).

3. **Limit interviews to agencies or organizations that offer positions for which you are truly qualified.**
   - ✓ Do a thorough self-assessment first.
   - ✓ Be enthusiastic about your experience and what you feel you could bring to the prospective position.
   - ✓ Be positive and truthful.
   - ✓ Project attentiveness and ask for clarification of anything you don't understand.
   - ✓ Show that you believe in yourself without boastfulness. Avoid self-deprecation.
   - ✓ Project self-respect and make it clear you will not compromise yourself just to get a job.
   - ✓ Never criticize a former employer.
   - ✓ Never accept a salary offer at the initial interview (if they really want you, you will find you have some leverage. Don't underestimate yourself).
   - ✓ Always follow up an interview with a thank-you letter.

4. **If it appears that you will not get a position:**
   - ✓ Inquire about perceived specific drawbacks that you may have inadvertently presented (to avoid doing this again.)
   - ✓ Ask what was viewed as being your strongest points.
   - ✓ Project your best professional impression; another position may become available to you in the future.
   - ✓ Don't become discouraged if you are not selected — it may mean that someone else was considerably more qualified or that their presentation was better.

TRAPS IN THE INTERVIEW

To best prepare yourself for "interview traps," consider some of the questions you are apt to face. What does the interviewer *really* want to know?

✦ **"Tell me about yourself"**
(Are you flexible, cooperative, liked by co-workers?)

✦ **"Which of your jobs did you enjoy most?"**
(Will our position be right for you? Will you thrive in this environment?)

✦ **"Can you travel or work overtime?"**
(Do you have family responsibilities that will interfere with your job?)

✦ **"Tell me about your leisure activities."**
(How much of your personal time or contacts may help us?)

✦ **"What would you say is your greatest strength?"**
(Are you confident or do you appear unsure of yourself?)

✦ **"What do you consider one of your weaknesses?"**
(In other words, can you accept constructive criticism? Show people you are capable of accepting a realistic appraisal of your actions and are interested in overcoming any weaknesses.)

✦ **"What are your future plans?"**
(Beware. They want to determine how long you expect to be with their organization.)

Generally speaking, a potential employer will not be interested in looking through your every certificate or award. But documenting your volunteer experiences could be the first step in developing a career portfolio. A complete record of your involvement will enable you to analyze the functions you can perform and the skills you have acquired.

Whenever possible avoid the personnel department. Determine the type of work you feel qualified to handle and seek out the individual who would become your supervisor . . . then sell yourself. The object is to create an image that says "I'm the person you've been looking for." Your demeanor in the interview, and the words you choose for your resumé, should all establish a picture of you as a capable, competent potential employee.

Appendix

". . . and in conclusion . . ."

The material included in the appendix seemed appropriate for a book on *Leadership Skills*, but somehow did not fit into any particular chapter. For this reason I am including these selections at the end. In each case, as with the material in the preceding chapters, these tools will only be helpful if you put them to use! Adapt, edit, revise, but use the enclosed material.

RESEARCH AND INTERVIEWING*

1. Types of Interview

✓ **Acquiring Information**
Seeking feedback, exploring issues, gathering data

✓ **Giving Information**
Sharing information, as in addressing a reporter

✓ **Advocating**
Modifying beliefs or attitudes, as in lobbying

✓ **Problem-Solving**
Resolving conflict or seeking solutions

2. Prepare

✓ **Do your Research**
The more you know before you go in, the more you are likely to know coming out

✓ **Establish what you are seeking**
Let your candidate know specifically what you are seeking, so he or she can be prepared.

✓ **Goals and objectives**
Establish goals and objectives for the session in advance.

✓ **Outline questions**
Do this ahead of time, but be flexible. Listen, be responsive, watch carefully and be prepared to modify your approach.

*Based on material by Susan Shultz, columnist, editor and executive search consultant (used with permission)

3. Before the Interview

✓ Define the information objectives

✓ Determine *who* you will interview

✓ Write your questions
  - Avoid ambiguous wording or biased direction
  - Keep questions conversational, simple and short
  - Avoid questions with two elements
  - Avoid loaded, biased questions
  - Consider the effects of one question on another

✓ Pre-test your questions when possible

✓ Contact the individual in advance
  - Precede your interview with a letter or phone call to indicate the range of questions and time needed
  - If your organization will be discussed during the interview, include a brochure and be prepared to answer the person's questions about it.

4. Create the Atmosphere

✓ Be fully prepared
  Be sure you know everything you need to know

✓ Establish a rapport.
  Make it easy for the person to talk to you

✓ Understand your position as interviewer
  Your job is primarily that of reporter. Take all opinions in your stride without surprise or disapproval

✓ Control
  Maintain control over the direction of the interview

✓ Remain impartial
  Be aware of your own biases and don't let them interfere

✓ Listen
  Let the person know you care about what he or she has to say

5. Type of Interview Questions

✓ Low-Structured Questions
  Questions calling for a specific response in a few words often begin with *Have, Are, Did, Will, Do.*

✓ High-Structured Questions
  Open-ended questions, designed to evoke more than enumerations or hard, concise facts. Usually begin *Like, How, What, Why, Tell.*

✓ Mirroring Questions
  Parroting to gain elaboration, nonjudgmental
  Usually a re-statement to keep the focus on the indvidual.

✓ Probe Questions
  Questions that bridge, in an attempt to probe for more depth
  A short statement such as *Why?* or *How is that?* designed to keep the person talking.

✓ Leading Questions
  Questions that strongly imply or encourage a specific answer. To confirm suspicions or test someone. Can be produced by words, tone of voice or an expression of bias.

✓ **Clarifying Questions**
Closure questions at the end of the interview to summarize; to ensure understanding of what the individual has said.
(*"Let me rephrase that . . ."*, *"As I understand it . . ."*,
"What I heard you say is . . .").

6. Record and Report

✓ **Check your notes**
Look for accuracy and thoroughness.
Make corrections immediately.

✓ **Reporting verbatim responses**
Often done to indicate attitudes, maintain meaning as well as emphasis

✓ **Report facts**
Separate facts from opinions and from your reactions in the written report. Draft your final report while your information is fresh.

✓ **Record**
- Record and make notes as the interview progresses.
- For accuracy, read back information if you are unsure.
- If appropriate, send a follow-up letter to the individual, summarizing any positions taken or commitments made.
- Clarify the use or information obtained in the interview.

The process is not finished until you have sent a note of thanks to the person sharing his or her time and knowledge with you.

Date your material, identify yourself as the author, and make a copy for yourself before sending it.

When To Probe
It is appropriate to use Probe Questions when the individual's response is.
- Inadequate, irrelevant or too vague
- Contradictory, or an avoidance of the Question
- Limited, incomplete, non-specific

GUIDELINES FOR PROPOSALS

State Clearly

- ✓ Your overall goal
- ✓ Your subsequent objectives
- ✓ Specifically what you propose to accomplish
- ✓ Why this is a significant goal and these are important objectives
- ✓ How you propose to accomplish your goal

Project Your Resource Expenditure

- ✓ How you will staff it (do it)?
- ✓ What is the time schedule for preparation and for the project itself?
- ✓ What will the line of authority and responsibility be?
- ✓ What resources do you have (such as money and material)?
- ✓ What additional resources will you need?

Measurable Results

Demonstrate for the reader how you plan to evaluate the results. Funding groups will want you to demonstrate how both the recipient of your service *and* your volunteers will gain something significant from this effort. *Measurable results* are the bottom line.

An impact on participants, as well as recipients, will help convince others of the overall value of your proposal. Demonstrating that your program will have an impact on participants—such as developing public-spirited, effective citizens with needed skills—will improve the image of your initiative. Impact on recipients is essential.

If your proposal is being made to a major corporation or government agency, consider using the help of a professional grant writer. The small investment could produce funding.

Potential Problems

Proposals are often turned down because of inadequacies in preparation. Here are reasons proposals are most often turned down:

- ✓ Your proposal will duplicate a service that already exists.
- ✓ Too much money will be allocated to administrative costs.
- ✓ Insufficient evidence is given that the project can sustain itself beyond the life of the funding or grant.
- ✓ The goals and objectives have not been clearly stated. It is not clear *how* it is to be implemented.
- ✓ The objectives do not coincide with those of the funding source.
- ✓ The monetary requirements of the project cannot be met by the agency approached.
- ✓ The proposal is poorly written and hard to understand.

Create a clean, neat, typed or computer-generated copy well in advance of the deadline. It should be double-spaced with wide margins. Provide pertinent supplementary material including a cover sheet, and a note as to who your contact person is.

If you are working on a smaller scale, the same general guidelines apply. Your final product may appear as a single sheet, such as a proposal for a fund-raiser prepared for consideration by your Board or general membership, but it should still spell out each of the key points listed.

REFERENCE FORM
VOLUNTEER WORK EXPERIENCE

VOLUNTEER:

Name:_____

Address:_____

Phone:_____

ORGANIZATION OR AGENCY SERVED:

Name:_____

Address:_____

Phone:_____

Supervisor: _____

VOLUNTEER JOB TITLE:

Describe skills, knowledge and abilities used to perform duties and responsibilities of the job (include tools and equipment used):

_____

_____

_____

_____

DATES OF SERVICE IN THIS VOLUNTEER POSITION: from:_____ to:_____

ACTUAL HOURS SERVED IN THIS JOB: per day _____ per week _____

per month_____ total hours _____

REASON FOR LEAVING THIS POSITION: _____

_____

SIGNATURE OF DIRECTOR OF VOLUNTEERS OR SUPERVISOR:

_____Date: _____

Name:_____

Title: _____

Address:_____

Phone:_____

Volunteer: Retain this form for your record. It is a documentation of your volunteer work experience and may be used as a job reference. Use a separate page for each position.

© 1994 Emily Kittle Morrison, *Leadership Skills*, Fisher Books, Tucson, Arizona

PROGRAM ADVERTISING

Beyond the profits of the door receipts from a sports tournament, cabaret or variety show, your Program is a great source of potential revenue. Here are suggestions on how to approach advertising.

- ✤ Start with friends of friends. List as many individuals and their firms as possible. This provides a personalized "in." Then:
    - ✓ Ask each to call or write to their contacts and to individually promote your cause. They will obviously require a Fact sheet, and guidelines regarding the specific requirements about such things as payment and camera-ready material for the advertisement.
    - ✓ You can compile a cross-reference list and assign a committee to prepare letters with a personal touch (i.e., "John Jones was sure you would want to place an ad in our program.") Itemize the specifics of the purchase of the ad, as well as who your market will be and how many you expect to reach.

- ✤ Send a follow-up letter with the specifics of your proposal. Word processors can personalize these letters.

- ✤ Within two weeks make follow-up phone call to discuss any questions, to make arrangements for getting the layout material to be used and to give another sales pitch.

- ✤ Stay away from the individuals in every firm programmed to say "no". Try by phone, when you have no "in," to determine who the best person is to talk to. Address your letter to that individual. Inquire when they set up their budget and how early you need to make your approach.

- ✤ Often a local advertising firm handles the companies that you are interested in attracting. They can make arrangements for you but will charge a percentage to their client.

- ✤ Charge what the market will bear, but remember your audience. Different events appeal to different individuals and thus become appealing to different advertisers. Some are more accustomed than others to paying steep prices for advertising.

- ✤ Consider sponsorships that allow the advertiser to have his product at your event, or to merchandise in some way in conjunction with the event. Some firms will not buy an ad unless they will be exclusive—such as no other soft-drink brand at the event.

- ✤ Once you are ready to prepare the final draft of your program, check around for volunteer assistance. Printing from camera-ready copy can save you thousands of dollars in "layout fees" (see Chapter 14, *Publicity*, for guidelines).

DESIGNING A QUESTIONNAIRE

Determine First

✓ What information is needed
✓ The type of questions to use
✓ The content of each question
✓ The wording of the question
✓ The sequence of the questions

Then

Design the layout and arrange for reproduction

✓ Pretest the questionnaire
✓ Revise and draft the final questionnaire

Considerations

✓ Content
  - Is the question really needed at all?
  - Are several questions needed instead of one?
  - Can the individual be expected to be knowledgeable or is he or she opinionated?
  - Can he be expected to answer the question (able to phrase and answer in writing, to share his information?)

✓ **Type of Questions**
  - Multiple choice—often none of the choices really fit; however, this approach may help the person focus. Easy to tabulate.
  - Dichotomous—two extremes such as "yes" or "no"
  - Open-ended— the person has a chance to answer in his own words; often more revealing (useful as a first question)
  - Scaled—such as 1 to 10 from *agree* to *disagree*. 1 to 5 would allow respondents to 'fence sit' on 3, always use an even number to force a choice.
  - Ranking—listing preferred choices in order
  - Never use a "leading question." These do not yield useful information.

✓ **Wording**
  - Remember the journalists' five *W's*: *who, what, where, when* and *why*. Occasionally *how* is also pertinent.
  - Avoid questions that may appear unreasonable to the person.
  - Never use "leading questions." These do not yield useful information.
  - Use simple words. Each word should have only one meaning.
  - Avoid ambiguous words that can be interpreted differently by different people (*frequently, normally, occasionally*).

✓ **Sequence**
  - Always design the first question to pique interest.
  - Remember that one question may have an effect on the response to another. Where possible, ask questions after the fact, so as not to bias the responses to the other question.
  - Hide difficult questions in the middle or end. As the person becomes involved in the process of answering, these should become easier to answer.
  - Follow a logical order. Think in terms of the person's viewpoint, where possible.

TIDBITS FROM TRAINING

✓ Date and identify any material you prepare.

✓ Keep at least one copy or the original of any material you entrust to mail or delivery services.

✓ People may all be looking at the same thing, but each person sees things differently.

✓ You get out of life what you put into it.

✓ Personal identity and fulfillment come from serving others.

✓ Have a Plan B.

✓ Get to know yourself; do what you enjoy most and do best.

✓ Look for the positive; deal graciously with the negative.

✓ If you do not plan to do it in the best way possible, don't say you will do it.

✓ Conflict should be resolved, not avoided.

✓ People remember only 30 percent of what they see and 20 percent of what they hear.

✓ Advance planning pays off in time saved in the end.

✓ Consider other people's needs.

✓ To find productive solutions, build a sense of a team with a common goal.

✓ Never call a meeting just to call a meeting

✓ State your expectations clearly in the beginning.

✓ If you don't manage your own time, someone less qualified will do it for you.

✓ Agendas should be specific. Time frames, topics and individual responsibilities should be spelled out.

✓ Decisions are no better than the information on which they are based.

✓ To evaluate is not to criticize, but to consider critically.

✓ Select the best time of day to tackle each task.

✓ If you do not do it right the first time, when will you have time to do it over?

✓ Use blank spaces in your day.

✓ When bogged down, move on to another project.

✓ A person's self-esteem is his most important possession.

✓ Make decisions at the lowest level possible.

✓ Take solutions, not problems, to the authority.

✓ Set realistic deadlines for yourself and others.

✓ Precede criticism with two words of praise.

✓ Surround and identify yourself with successful people.

✓ Find solutions, not fault (or blame).

STEPS IN MAKING A PRESENTATION

Five Elements of a Presentation
- ✓ Pre-presentation
- ✓ The Beginning
- ✓ The Body
- ✓ The End
- ✓ Post-presentation analysis

The Pre-Presentation
- ✓ Examine the five *W's*
  - *Who?* May include:
      Presenters—trainers or facilitators
      Participants—all those who will be receiving the presentation
      Others—anyone else whose views or input will influence the presentation
  - *What?* The subject to be covered in the presentation
  - *Why?* Clearly define objectives for the session
  - *Where?* Location (all environmental factors should be examined)
  - *When?* Date and time
- ✓ **Planning begins with analysis of the answers to the five W's**
  - Have reasonable objectives been set?
  - What background and experience will audience have?
  - What do they expect from the session?
  - What is the scope and depth of the material to be covered?
  - What resources are available for use in the presentation?
  - What background and ability are you, the presenter, providing?
  - What limitations are involved? (time, space, etc.)
- ✓ **Formalizing—develop the specifics of the plan**
  - Do you have an agenda and workable time frame?
  - Have you defined participant activities and responsibilities, if there are any?
- ✓ **Preparing—take care of details**
  - Have you completed all handouts, guides, references, etc.?
  - Have you confirmed all coordinating elements?
  - Have you practiced with equipment—A.V. (Audio Visuals), public address systems, etc.? Are spare lamps or spare equipment available in case of breakdowns?
  - Have you held a critiqued rehearsal to evaluate both content and delivery?
  - Have you arrived early enough to check and/or adjust any on-site preparation?

Beginning
- ✓ **The presenter has four minutes to create the climate!**
  - You must command audience attention. Don't rely on the introduction you have been given.
  - Choose a method that is comfortable for you and appropriate to the situation
- ✓ **Pay attention to style**
  - Notes—what kind are best for you? (3 x 5 cards, 'ghost writing' lightly in pencil to guide you as you make the chart in front of your audience.)

- Gear your vocabulary to the group, but don't talk down
- Avoid mannerisms that could be distracting

✓ **Establish the fundamentals of the presentation**
  - State the objectives, for approval
  - Establish any other conditions or ground rules (norms)
  - Relate presentation to any preceding or subsequent presentations

✓ **Stimulate the participants to activity**
(must be done early in the session)

The Body ✓ **Fundamental methods**
  - Telling or lecturing
  - Showing or demonstrating
  - Participating
    Brainstorming—controlled process to stimulate creativity.
    Discussion—presenter as facilitator.
    Buzz Groups—discussion groups reach consensus.
    Case Study—hypothetical situation.
    Role Playing—participants act out a given situation .
    Dyads, Triads—groups of 2 or 3 people who perform a task.
    Exercises—any structured activity that relates to the presentation.

✓ **Feedback**
  - Be aware of both verbal and non-verbal reaction
  - Watch the process
  - Use clarifying techniques—"What I hear you saying . . ."
  - Be aware of any environmental factors
  - Be flexible

The Ending ✓ **Should be planned and prepared but should be adjusted to reflect feedback**
  - Summarize
  - Relate parts to the whole
  - Reinforce key points

Post-Presentation Analysis ✓ **Conduct an evaluation—written, verbal or both**

✓ **Were the objectives met?**
  - What factors contributed to success? Build these into future presentations (Preserve)
  - What factors could be improved upon (Improve)
  - What factors detracted? Eliminate or neutralize these

✓ **Revise and refine the presentation**

**LIABILITIES
For Non-profit
Associations**

Any time an organization incorporates, it enters a new category in terms of liability. It is important that the Articles of Incorporation contain provisions for mandatory indemnification of Board members.

Your name on a letterhead can place you in liability. Insurance against officer and director liability is, unfortunately, a must.

A non-profit organization takes on the same powers as other corporations. That implies it can contract, sue, be sued, own property and continue to exist independent of any one person. It has a separate legal identity and its liability is limited to the corporation's assets.

The non-profit corporation must be governed by a Board of Directors with fiduciary responsibility. These Directors must answer to the corporation, its members, and the state attorney general. This includes compliance with all IRS and other federal and state requirements. Directors may be held accountable even for acts committed in ignorance of the law.

Special care should be taken when accepting federal and state grant money. Government rules are easy to overlook and misunderstand. Miscalculations can be costly. Here it is especially important to have qualified legal and accounting counsel. If a corporation cannot account for grant funds it receives, each board member may be held liable for the full amount! Accepting any grant money means entering into a contractual obligation.

One of the best ways to minimize risks is to have an annual audit by a certified public accountant. ("Certified" because they carry malpractice insurance) It is a responsibility of the Board to select a qualified CPA to serve as an independent source of information.

Corporations should carry liability insurance covering activities of their members, even on errands for the organization. Volunteers are, in fact, "gratuitous employees" when they are performing under direction and supervision of organizational or agency officers. The extent of the corporate and individual liability should be clearly spelled out. Expectations of the Board members must be well defined.

The obligation to exercise due care means each Director is liable for any losses the corporation may suffer through negligence, though not error in judgment, if the director can show he acted in good faith.

Each Board member should be fully informed of his or her liability when accepting a position as Director with any corporation, even nonprofit.

Provisions should be made in Bylaws for the automatic removal of a director who does not participate or who behaves in a manner inconsistent with the policies of the Board because this can create liabilities for the organization and its Board.

When a meeting is held, and parliamentary procedure is essential, the following form can be very helpful.

PARLIAMENTARY PROCEDURE AT A GLANCE

To Do This	You Say This	May You Interrupt the Speaker?	Must You Be Seconded?	Is The Motion Debatable?	What Vote Is Required?
Adjourn the meeting*	"I move that we adjourn"	No	Yes	No	Majority
Recess the meeting	"I move that we recess until . . .	No	Yes	No	Majority
Complain about noise, room temp. etc.*	"Point of privilege"	Yes	No	No	No vote
Suspend further consideration of something"*	"I move that we table it"	No	Yes	No	Majority
End debate	"I move we vote on the previous question"	No	Yes	No	2/3 vote
Postpone consideration of something	"I move we postpone this matter until"	No	Yes	Yes	Majority
Have something studied further	"I move we refer matter to a committee".	No	Yes	Yes	Majority
Amend a motion	"I move that this motion be amended by"	No	Yes	Yes	Majority
Introduce business (a primary motion)	"I move that . . ."	No	Yes	Yes	Majority
Object to procedure or to a personal affront*	"Point of Order"	Yes	No	No	Chair decides
Request information*	"Point of information"	Yes	No	No	No vote
Ask for a vote by actual count to verify a voice vote*	"I call for a division" of the house"	No	No	No	No vote
Object to considering some undiplomatic item	"I object to consideration of this question"	Yes	No	No	2/3 vote
Take up a matter previously tabled*	"I move to take from the table"	No	Yes	No	Majority
Reconsider something already disposed of*	"I move we reconsider our action relative to"	Yes	Yes	Yes	Majority
Consider something out of its scheduled order*	"I move we suspend the rules and consider"	Yes	Yes	No	2/3 vote
Vote on a ruling by the chair*	"I appeal the chair's decision	Yes	Yes	Yes	Majority

* Not Amendable

© 1994 Emily Kittle Morrison, *Leadership Skills*, Fisher Books, Tucson, Arizona

Suggested Readings

Voluntarism Brown, Kathleen M, *Keys To Making a Volunteer Program Work*, Arden Publications, Richmond, CA, 1982

Do It Voluntarily, Junior League of San Diego, 1978

Ellis, S. J. and K. J. Noyes, *By The People: A History of Americans*, San Francisco, CA, Oxford, 1990.

Fessler, Donald R., *Facilitating Community Change*, University Associates, La Jolla, CA., 1976

Hanlon, Brenda, *The Best of Val*, The National Center For Citizen Involvement, Washington, DC, 1980

Hodgkinson, V. A. and Weitzmer, M.S., *Giving and Volunteering in The United States*, The Independent Sector, Washington, D.C., 1988.

Flanagan, Joan, *The Successful Volunteer Organization*, Chicago Books, Inc., Chicago, IL 1981

I Can, American Red Cross, 1981

Lewis, C. O., Leo F. Johnson, *Keys to Creative Work With Volunteers*, Worcester, MA.

Naylor, Harriet H., *Volunteers Today*, Dryden, NY., 1973

Scheitlin, George, and Eleanore L. Gillstrom, Recruiting and *Developing Volunteer Leaders*, Parish Life Press, Philadelphia PA 1973

Sochen, June, *Movers and Shakers*, Quadrangle/New York Times Book Co., 1974

Stone, Julita Martinez, *How To Volunteer in Social Service Agencies*, Charles C. Thomas, Springfield, IL, 1982

Meetings Bradford, Leland P., *Making Meetings Work*, University Associates, La Jolla, CA, 1976

Daniels, William R., *Orchestrating Powerful Regular Meetings*, Pfeiffer and Co., San Diego, CA, 1990

Doyle, Michael, and David Straus, *How To Make Meetings Work,* Wyden, NY, 1976

Lawson, John D., *When You Preside,* Interstate Printers & Publishers, Danville, IL, 1980

Schindler-Rinman, Eva, and Ronald Lippitt, *Taking Your Meetings Out of the Doldrums,* University Associates, La Jolla, CA.

Board Skills   Harshmen, Carl L., and Phillips, Steven L., *Teaming Up,* Pfeiffer and Co., San Diego, 1994

Harshman, Carl L., *The Non-Profit Board,* O'Connell, 1981

The Nonprofit Board in 1983, *Voluntary Action Leadership,* Arlington, VA., 1983

Nordhoff, Nancy S., et al. *Fundamental Practices for Success With Volunteer Boards for Non-Profit Organizations,* 1983

O'Connell, Brian, *Effective Leadership in Voluntary Organizations,* Follett Publishing, Chicago, IL, 1981

Wilson, Marlene, *Effective Management of Volunteer Programs,* Volunteer Management Associates, Boulder, CO., 1979

Group Process   Aldrich, Howard E., *Organizations and Environments,* Prentice Hall, Inc., Englewood Cliffs, NY, 1979

Berne, E., *Games People Play,* Grove Press, NY., 1964

Bion, W.R., *Experiences in Groups,* Ballentine, NY., 1975

Egan, Gerald, *Encounter: Group Process for Interpersonal Growth,* Brooks/ Cole Publishing Co., Belmont, CA, 1970

Keirsay, David and Bates, Marilyn, *Please Understand Me,* Prometheus Nemesis Book Co., Del Mar, CA, 1984

Leadership   Beal, George M., Joe Bohlen & J. Neil Raudabaugh, *Leadership & Dynamic Group Action,* Iowa State University Press, Ames, IA, 1962

Bemmis, Warren, *On Becoming a Leader,* Addison Wesley Publishing, NY, 1989

Bothwell, Lin, *The Art of Leadership,* Prentice Hall Press, NY, NY, 1988

Burke, W. Warner, *Interpersonal Communications,* in William Lassey and Richard R. Fernandez, (Eds), *Leadership and Social Change,* University Associates, La Jolla, CA., 1976

Drucker, Peter, *The Effective Executive,* Morrow, NY, NY, 1972

Fox, W. and Penrod, K., *A Vision For Strenghtening Local Leadership,* Perdue University, Cooperative Extension Service, 1989

Lawson, Leslie Griffin, et al, *Lead On!,* Impact Publishers, San Luis Obispo, CA, 1982

Lundy, James, Ph D., *Lead, Follow or Get Out of the Way,* Pfeiffer and Co. San Diego, CA, 1993

Pegg, Mike, *Positive Leadership,* Pfeiffer and Co., San Diego, CA, 1994

Seita, T. *Leadership Skills for the New Age of Non-Profits*, Heritage Arts, Downers Grove IL, 1990

Silver, N. *At the Heart*, Valley Volunteer Center, Pleasanton, CA 1988

Motivation

Anderson, Richard, Motivation: *The Master Key*, Correan Publications, Los Gatos, CA, 1973

Carnegie, Dale, *How To Win Friends and Influence People*, Pocket Books, NY, 1936

Ford, Edward, and Robert Zorn, *Why Be Lonely*, Argus Communications, Niles, IL, 1975

Glasser, W., F., *Reality Therapy*, Harper & Row, NY, 1965

Kroeger, Otto, and huesen, Janet M., *Type Talk*, Tilden Press Book, NY, NY, 1989

Levin, Stanley, "How to Motivate Volunteers", *Volunteers in Rehabilitation*, Washington, D.C., Goodwill Industries of America, Inc., 1973, Booklet #9

Luthans, F., and R. Kreitner, *Organizational Behavior Modification*, Scott Forsman, Glenview, IL, 1975

McClelland, D.C. (ED.), *Human Motivation*, General Learning Press, Morristown, N.J., 1973

Maslow, Abraham, *Motivation & Personality*, Harper and Row, NY, 1954

Pell, Arthur R., *Recruiting, Training & Motivating Volunteer Workers*, Pilot Books, NY, 1972

Peter, Dr. Lawrence J., *The Peter Principle*, Morrow, NY, NY, 1972

Communication

Erikson, Karin, *Communication Skills for Human Services*, Reston Publishing, 1979

Fast, Julius, *Body Language*, M. Evans & Co., Inc., c/o J.B. Lippincott, Philadelphia, PA, 1970

Miller, Sherod, *Alive and Aware: Improving Communication in Relationships*, Minneapolis, MN, 1975

Mortensen, D. David, Communication, *The Study of Interaction*, McGraw Hill, NY, 1972

Myers, Isabel Briggs and Myers, Peter B., *Gifts Differing*, Consulting Psychologists' Press Inc., Palo Alto, CA, 1980

Listening

Adler, Mortimer J., *How to Speak, How to Listen*, MacMillian, NY, 1983

Erikson, Karin, *Communication Skills for Human Services*, Reston Publishing, Co., 1979

Hayakawa, S.I., *Language in Thought and Action*, Harcourt, Brace & World, NY, 1964

Problem-Solving

Adams, James, *Conceptual Blockbusting, A Guide To Better Ideas*, W.W. Norton & Co., Inc., NY, 1979

deBono, Edward, *New Think*, N.Y. Basic Books, 1967

Kaufman, Roger, *Identifying and Solving Problems: A System Approach*

Maltz, Maxwell, *Psycho Cybernetics*, Prentice-Hall, NY, 1960

Osborn, Alex, *Applied Imagination*, Scribner, NY, 1979

Patton, Bobby R., and Kim Giffin, *Problem Solving and Group Interaction*, Harper and Row, NY, 1973

Peck, M. Scot, M.D., *The Road Less Traveled*, A Touchstone Book, NY, 1978

Straus, David, *Participatory Decision Making*, AMACOM, NY, 1974

Tuchnan, Bruce, *Conducting Educational Research*, Harcourt, Brace, Jananovich, San Francisco, CA, 1972

Time Management

Bliss, Edwin, *Getting Things Done*, the ABC's of Time Management

Covey, Stephen, *Seven Habits of Highly Effective People*, Simon & Schuster, NY, *1989*

Ferner, Jack D., *Successful Time Management*, John Wiley and Sons, NY, NY., 1980

Hobbs, Charles R., *Insight on Time Management*, Charles R. Hobbs Corp., Salt Lake City UT, 1978

Lakein, Alan, *How To Get Control of Your Time and Your Life*, Peter H. Wyden, Inc., N.Y, 1973

MacKenzie, R.A., *Managing Time at the Top*, The Presidents Association, NY, 1970

MacKenzie, R.A., *New Time Management Methods*, The Dartnell Corp., Chicago, IL, 1975

Quality Management

Brudney, Jeffrey, *Fostering Volunteer Programs in the Public Sector*, San Francisco, CA Jossey-Bass, 1990.

Crosby, Philip B., *The Art of Getting Your Own Sweet Way*, McGraw Hill, NY, 1972

Drucker, Peter, *Managing the Non-Profit Organization*, Harper Business, NY, NY, 1990

Ellis, S. J., *From the Top Down: The Executive Role in Volunteer Program Success*, Energize, PA, 1986

Hanson, Pauline, *The Board Member—Decision Maker for the Non-Profit Corporation*

LeBoeuf, M., *Working Smart*, McGraw-Hill, NY, 1979

Naylor, H., *Beyond Managing Volunteers*, Yellow Fire Press, Boulder, CO, 1986

Nolan et al, Timothy, PhD, *Plan or Die*, Pfeiffer and Company, San Diego, CA, 1993

McConkey, Dale B., *How To Manage By Results*, 3rd ed., AMACOM, NY

O'Connell, Brinn, *Effective Leadership in Voluntary Organiztions*, Follett Publishing, Chicago, IL, 1976

Scott, Cynthia, PhD., and Jagge, Dennis T., PhD., *Managing Organizational Change*, Crisp Publications, Inc., Los Altos, CA, 1989.

Tosi, Henry L., and Jerald W. Young, *Management, Experiences and Demonstrations*, Richard D. Irwin, Inc., Homewood, IL, 1980

Wilson, Marlene, T*he Effectiue Management of Volunteer Programs*, Volunteer Management Associates, Boulder, CO, 1979

Conflict Management

Cohen, Herb, *You Can Negotiate Anything*, Stuart, Secaucus, N.J., 1980

Hart, Lois B, *Learning from Conflict*, Addison Wesley Publishing Co., Reading, MA, 1981

Kniveton, Broomley, *Training For Negotiating*, Business Books, London, 1978

McCurley, S, Vineyard, S., *101 Ideas for Volunteer Programs*, Heritage Arts Publishers, 1986

Waitley, Denis, *The Double Win*, Fleming H. Revell Co, Old Tappan, NJ 1982

Weisinger, Dr. Hendrie, and Lobsenz, Norman M., *Nobody's Perfect (How to Give Criticism and Get Results)*, Wamer Books, NY 1983

Self-Assessment/ Group Assessment

Campbell, David, *If You Don't Know Where You're Going, You'll Probably End up Somewhere Else*, Argus Communications, Niles, IL 1974

Downey, Darcy Campion, *The Volunteer's Survival Manual*, Practical Press, MA, 1992

Helas, Celia, and Roherta Matteson, *I've Done So Well, Why Do I Feel So Bad?* MacMillan, NY, 1977

Harragan, Lehan, *Games Mother Never Taught You*, Rawson Associates, NY, 1977

Howell, Mary C., *Helping Ourselves*, Beacon Press, Boston, MA, 1975

Kiev, Ari, M.D., *A Strategy for Success*, MacMillan, NY, 1977

Kurtz, Paul, *Exuberance*, Prometheus Books, Buffalo, NY, 1977

Newman, Mildred, and Bernard Berkowitz, *How to Take Charge of Your Life*, Bantam, NY, 1978

Newman, Mildred, and Bernard Berkowitz, *How to to Your Own Best Friend*, Ballantine, NY, 1975

Roges, Carl, *On Becoming a Person*, Houghton Mifflin Company, Boston, MA, 1961

Sheehy, Gail *Passages*, Bantam, NY, 1984

Steiner, Claud M., *Scripts People Live: Transactional Analysis of Life Scripts*, Grove Press, NY, 1974

Weinberg, Dr. George, *Self Creation*, Avon, NY, 1978

Publicity

Delacorte, Toni, *How to Get Free Press*, G. P. Putman's Sons, S.F., CA, 1981

Hall, Babette, *The Right Angles, How to Do Successful Publicity*, I. Wasburn, NY, 1965

Gee, B., *Winning the Image Game*, The Free Press, Berkeley CA, NY, 1989

Kotler, P. and Roberto, E, *Social Marketing*, The Free Press, NY, 1989

Kurtz, Harold, *Public Relations and Fund Raising for Hospitals*, Thomas, Springfield, IL., 1981

Mallory, Charles, *Publicity Power*, Crisp Publications, Los Altos, CA, 1989

Career Development

Bolles, Richard, *What Color Is Your Parachute?* Ten Speed Press, Berkeley, 1972

Eisen, Jeffrey, *Get The Right Job Now*, Lippincott, NY, 1978

Pader, Shirley, *From Kltchen to Career*, Stein and Day, NY., 1977

Jame, Muriel and Jongeward, Dorothy, *Born To Win*, Addison Wesley Publishing, Reading MA, 1976

Haldane, Bernard, *Career Satisfaction and Success*, AMACOM, NY, 1974

Lobb, Charlotte, *Exploring Careers Through Volunteerism*, Rosen, NY, 1976

Sinetar, Marsha, *Do What You Love and the Money will Follow*, Dell, NY, NY, 1989

—*Volunteer Skills Portfolio: Passport to the Paid Workplace*, Association of Junior Leagues, Inc. 1981

Scholz, Nell Tumlin, Judith Sosebee Prince, Cordon Porter Miller, *How To Decide—A Workbook for Women*, Avon Books, 1975

Yaeger, Neil, *Career Map: Deciding What you Want, Getting It and Keeping It*, John Wiley and Sons, NY, 1979

Index